A Question of Thinking

A First Look at Students' Performance on Open-ended Questions in Mathematics

 Publishing Information

A Question of Thinking: A First Look at Students' Performance on Open-ended Questions in Mathematics was compiled by staff from the California Assessment Program, California Department of Education, and was published by the Department, 721 Capitol Mall, Sacramento, California (mailing address: P.O. Box 944272, Sacramento, CA 94244-2720).

The document was distributed under the provisions of the Library Distribution Act and *Government Code* Section 11096.

© Copyright 1989, California Department of Education

Copies of this publication are available for $6 each, plus sales tax for California residents, from the Bureau of Publications, Sales Unit, California Department of Education, P.O. Box 271, Sacramento, CA 95812-0271.

A list of other publications available from the Department may be found on pages 83–84, or a complete list may be obtained by writing to the address given above or by calling (916) 445-1260.

ISBN 0-8011-0815-2

Contents

Preface v
Acknowledgments vii

Part I: Open-ended Questions in Mathematics 1
    Description of the Mathematics Portion of the Grade Twelve Test 3
    Developing Open-ended Questions 3
    Scoring Students' Responses 3
    Reporting Results 4
    Future Plans 5
    Summary of Students' Performance on the Open-ended Questions 5

Part II: Discussion of Results 7
    Problem A 7
        General Expectations 7
        Strengths and Weaknesses in Students' Responses 8
        Summary of Results and Instructional Implications 12
    Problem B 13
        General Expectations 13
        Strengths and Weaknesses in Students' Responses 14
        Summary of Results and Instructional Implications 21
    Problem C 21
        General Expectations 21
        Strengths and Weaknesses in Students' Responses 22
        Summary of Results and Instructional Implications 28
    Problem D 29
        General Expectations 29
        Strengths and Weaknesses in Students' Responses 29
        Summary of Results and Instructional Implications 35
    Problem E 36
        General Expectations 36
        Strengths and Weaknesses in Students' Responses 36
        Summary of Results and Instructional Implications 42

Part III: Scoring Students' Responses to Open-ended Questions in Mathematics 44
    Development of Scoring Rubrics 44
    Procedure for Developing Your Own Rubrics 46
    1987–88 Individual Scoring Rubrics for Problems A Through E 46
    Scoring Rubric for Problem A 47
    Scoring Rubric for Problem B 48
    Scoring Rubric for Problem C 49
    Scoring Rubric for Problem D 50
    Scoring Rubric for Problem E 52
    Generalized Rubric 53

Part IV: Additional Responses and Problems 54
    Sample Scored 1987 Responses 54
    Sample Scored 1988 Responses 64
    Additional Open-ended Problems 74

Preface

What is tested is what gets taught. Tests must measure what is most important.[1]

The California Assessment Program (CAP) is committed to aligning its assessment practices with the concepts presented in the *Mathematics Framework for California Public Schools: Kindergarten Through Grade Twelve*,[2] the *Mathematics Model Curriculum Guide: Kindergarten Through Grade Eight*,[3] and such publications as the *Curriculum and Evaluation Standards* published by the National Council of Teachers of Mathematics.[4] Educators as well as the public believe that the influence of assessment on the curriculum greatly affects the classroom teaching and learning processes.

Open-ended questions in mathematics (those requiring a written response, as opposed to multiple choice) have the potential to drive the curriculum in positive directions sought by leaders in education. The written responses required by open-ended mathematics questions stimulate students to think about mathematical problems and enable the students to communicate their mathematical thinking and solutions to others. When teachers can see students' thought processes sketched out in some detail, they can then target instruction appropriately to develop students' thinking further.

This report is the first large-scale attempt to discover how students think about and use mathematics. Readers will find that questions posed to students were written to stimulate their higher-level thinking processes (e.g., to make assumptions, see connections among strands of mathematics, explain to an audience, use data organization and graphing, and understand mathematical procedures). The examples illustrated in this report should serve as a powerful medium to learn about students' levels of accomplishment as well as methods for positively influencing classroom instruction in mathematics.

---

[1] *Everybody Counts: A Report to the Nation on the Future of Mathematics Education.* Washington, D.C.: National Academy Press, 1989, p. 69.
[2] *Mathematics Framework for California Public Schools: Kindergarten Through Grade Twelve.* Sacramento: California State Department of Education, 1985.
[3] *Mathematics Model Curriculum Guide: Kindergarten Through Grade Eight.* Sacramento: California State Department of Education, 1987.
[4] *Curriculum and Evaluation Standards for School Mathematics.* Reston, Va.: National Council of Teachers of Mathematics, 1989.

Many educators have contributed to the development of questions and to the preparation of this report. Although the Mathematics Assessment Advisory Committee provided much of the innovative thinking, many other educators serving on the ad hoc committees contributed to the improvement of the content of this report. The names of the Mathematics Assessment Advisory Committee members and members who served on the ad hoc rubrics development and scoring committee are given in the Acknowledgments. The Department wishes to thank these professionals, who gave their talents generously to improve assessment practices. We also thank the school districts that willingly provided release time for many of these educators.

We suggest that readers try a few of the questions before reading students' responses. This approach will give an idea of the thinking involved in answering the questions. Since this is the first report of its kind, we encourage readers to provide comments about assessment through the use of open-ended questions or about any other aspect of this report. Questions should be directed to Tej Pandey or Kathie Scott of the California Assessment Program (916-657-3011).

JAMES R. SMITH
Deputy Superintendent
Curriculum and Instructional Leadership

FRANCIE ALEXANDER
Associate Superintendent; and Director,
Curriculum, Instruction, and Assessment Division

DALE CARLSON
Assistant Superintendent
California Assessment Program

Acknowledgments

This report was developed by the members of the Mathematics Assessment Advisory Committee and special advisers.

Assessment Advisory Committee Members

Nicholas Branca
San Diego State University

Leigh Childs
Office of the San Diego County
　Superintendent of Schools

Larry Chrystal
University of California, Irvine

Clyde L. Corcoran
The Claremont Graduate School
　Teacher Internship Program

Brenda Gentry-Norton
Lemon Grove Middle School

Ana Golan
Santa Ana Unified School District

Donna Goldenstein
Hayward Unified School District

Elois M. Irvin
Kennedy High School, Richmond

Robin Kato
Jose Ortega Elementary School, San Francisco

Roberta Koss
Redwood High School, Larkspur

Judy Kysh
University of California, Davis

Kathy Layton
Beverly Hills High School

Sandra Marshall
San Diego State University

Clarita Montalban
Jurupa Unified School District

Ruth Parker
Office of the Alameda County
　Superintendent of Schools

Annie Podesto
Stockton City Unified School District

Gail Robinette
Fresno Unified School District

Alan Schoenfeld
University of California, Berkeley

Jean Stenmark
EQUALS, Lawrence Hall of Science
University of California, Berkeley

Ric Thomas
Office of the Los Angeles County
　Superintendent of Schools

Julian Weissglass
University of California, Santa Barbara

Les Winters
Los Angeles Unified School District

Special Advisers

Joan Akers
Mathematics, Science, and Environmental
  Education Unit
California State Department of Education

Agnes Bailey
Sacramento High School

Philip Daro
University of California, Berkeley

Carol Dean
Pasadena City College (retired)

Richard Dean
California Institute of Technology, Pasadena
  (retired)

Walter Denham
Office of Mathematics, Science, Health,
  Nutrition, and Physical Education
California State Department of Education

Tom Dodd
Fowler High School

Joan Gell
University of California, Los Angeles

Don Gernes
Ponderosa High School, Shingle Springs

Rowena Hacker
Trabuco Hills High School, Mission Viejo

Ken Johnson
Sacramento High School

Chuc Kemesu
Castlemont Senior High School, Oakland

Carol Langbort
San Francisco State University

Steve Lege
Davis Senior High School

Thomas Lester
Mathematics, Science, and
  Environmental Education Unit
California State Department of Education

Joseph Lipson
California State University, Chico

Irvin Peckham
University of California, San Diego

Sharon Ross
California State University, Chico

G. Thomas Sallee
University of California, Davis

Beth Schlesinger
San Diego Senior High School

Elizabeth Stage
EQUALS, Lawrence Hall of Science
University of California, Berkeley

Troy Thompson
Williams High School

Bob Tieslau
Amador High School, Sutter Creek

Jerry Vander Beek
Golden Sierra High School, Garden Valley

Dorothy Wood
Redwood High School, Larkspur

Principal support in developing this document was provided by Tej Pandey, Mathematics and Science Coordinator, California Assessment Program.

California Assessment Program staff who contributed to the preparation are Kathy Comfort, Gary Konas, James Miller, Kristin Palmquist, and Kathie Scott.

Part I

Open-ended Questions in Mathematics

Open-ended questions were included in the grade twelve mathematics test of the California Assessment Program (CAP) for the first time in 1987–88. This report describes the rationale for adding these questions. More important, what was learned from students' responses to the open-ended questions is described and related to ideas for improving classroom instruction.

The multiple-choice portion of the grade twelve mathematics test was changed to align it with the concepts presented in the *Mathematics Framework for California Public Schools: Kindergarten Through Grade Twelve* and in the *Model Curriculum Standards: Grades Nine Through Twelve*.[1] Seventy percent of the questions on the revised test involved problem solving and applications, and the remaining items tested understanding of mathematical concepts and principles.

The inclusion of open-ended questions is part of CAP's long-standing emphasis on aligning assessment with principles from the California curriculum frameworks. Open-ended questions were intended to improve the grade twelve test's alignment with the concepts presented in the 1985 *Framework* in the following ways:

CAP emphasizes aligning assessment with principles from the curriculum frameworks.

- Open-ended questions provide students an opportunity to think for themselves and to express their mathematical ideas that are consistent with their mathematical development.

- Open-ended questions call for students to construct their own responses instead of choosing a single answer.

Students construct their own responses instead of choosing a single answer.

- Open-ended questions allow students to demonstrate the depth of their understanding of a problem, almost an impossibility with multiple-choice items.

---

[1] *Model Curriculum Standards: Grades Nine Through Twelve.* Sacramento: California State Department of Education, 1985.

. . . open-ended questions

- Open-ended questions encourage students to solve problems in many ways, in turn reminding teachers to use a variety of methods to "get across" mathematical concepts.

- Open-ended questions model an important ingredient of good classroom instruction: openness to diverse responses to classroom questioning and discussion. Similarly, open-ended questions in assessment help educators move away from a curriculum of bits and pieces of information to a curriculum where students apply a set of mathematical tools as they are appropriate to situations.

Since the use of open-ended questions to assess students' knowledge of mathematics is new in California, this portion of the 1987–88 *Survey of Academic Skills, Grade 12* served as a pilot to inform educators about the introduction of new kinds of tasks in future CAP assessments. A subcommittee of the Mathematics Assessment Advisory Committee developed the open-ended questions and prepared this report on students' responses.

By writing freely about problems, students can discover solutions.

By presenting open-ended questions that required written responses, the committee sought to gain evidence for the importance of writing in the mathematics curriculum. Good mathematics teachers have learned that writing is both a way of thinking and of communicating. By writing freely about problems, students often can discover solutions. By reporting their methods in writing, students can tell others how to solve problems. By reading what students have written, teachers can gain more informed insights into students' knowledge and possible misconceptions, compared with what teachers learn from seeing only students' mathematical computations or answers.

We invite you as classroom teachers to read this report and to consider how you might use open-ended questions in your instruction. We suggest that you go through the booklet at least twice. The first time, you may want to browse through the students' answers to get a sense of the range of responses. The second time, try going back to read the committee's expectations for responses to each problem and the ways in which students went astray. See whether you agree with our recommendations for mathematics instruction directed toward addressing students' misconceptions.

We also urge you to try these open-ended questions and many others with your own students. We believe that you will be convinced, as was the committee, that students clearly need more experience with situation-oriented open-ended problems.

Description of the Mathematics Portion of the Grade Twelve Test

The mathematics section of the 1987–88 version of the twelfth grade CAP test consisted of 360 multiple-choice and five open-ended questions. Each student was asked to answer 11 multiple-choice questions (one without calculators and ten with calculators allowed) and one open-ended question. Although there was no strict time limit for students to answer questions, approximately 15 minutes were allowed for the multiple-choice items and 12 minutes for the single open-ended question.

Developing Open-ended Questions

In developing open-ended questions, the committee faced decisions regarding the structure of the items. A tightly structured question is easily scored but yields little interesting information about mathematical understanding. A broadly structured question allows students to respond creatively, demonstrate the full extent of their mathematical understanding, and display the elegance and originality of their thought processes. The committee struggled with this dichotomy and decided to try out a variety of questions, from tightly structured to somewhat broadly structured. Of the five questions described in this report, questions B and E have tight structures, whereas questions A, C, and D have relatively broad structures.

Scoring Students' Responses

Open-ended questions can be scored in several ways. Two frequently used methods of scoring students' writing are *analytic* and *holistic*. In analytic scoring, the evaluator considers whether specific points have been addressed in the student's response. A student is scored according to the points that have been satisfactorily covered. In holistic scoring, judgment is based on the response as a whole rather than on specific features of the response. Thus students' essays or responses are assembled in several stacks from low to high, according to the levels of the responses. Holistic scoring focuses on the merits of the response as a whole, rather than on how well the writing conforms to predetermined analytic schemes. Scoring holistically leaves the evaluator free, as we hope a teacher would be, to respond to the student's entire thinking process rather than concentrate on the number of points to be marked off according to a scheme.

Scoring holistically allows for a response to the entire thinking process.

. . . scoring students' responses

Implicitly, with holistic scoring more responsibility is placed on the student to determine the important elements of the question, providing opportunities for students to respond creatively. With analytic scoring the assumption is that questions have been well structured for the student and elicit well-defined patterns of student behavior.

For the convenience of classroom teachers who develop their own open-ended questions and wish to score students' responses to them, we have provided a general scoring rubric. Please refer to page 53 in Part III of the report for a rubric or rule that outlines criteria for scoring open-ended mathematics questions, in general.

Reporting Results

The committee reviewed a random sample of 2,500 responses, approximately 500 responses to each of the five questions, out of a total of 240,000 responses from twelfth grade students statewide. Since funding was provided to score only a sample of responses, there were not enough responses from which to compute school-by-school results. Therefore, this report reflects only the statewide performance on the open-ended questions. A "Summary of Students' Performance on the Open-ended Questions" appears on page 5 of the report.

Open-ended questions can test students' understanding and help teachers improve math instruction.

This booklet was assembled to report the results of the 1987–88 pilot test of open-ended questions in such a way that teachers will perceive their utility both for testing students' understanding and for improving mathematics instruction. Thus students' responses to each of the five open-ended questions, problems A, B, C, D, and E (students' "papers"), are described in the following format:

- A statement of the problem is given.

- "General Expectations" presents the committee's expectations for students' responses to the problem; for example:
    - What does the problem require, and how do we expect the students to work out a solution?
    - What elements of the problem relate to the *Mathematics Framework*?

- "Strengths and Weaknesses in Student Responses" examines:
    - What approaches led students to solve the problem?

– What difficulties prevented students from reaching a good solution?

This section presents an examination of the students' misconceptions and a description of teaching implications which suggest instructional strategies to overcome students' difficulties.

- "Summary of Results and Instructional Implications" provides the percentages of students who answered correctly or incorrectly and contains a summary of the implications for teaching learned from detailed examination of students' misconceptions and correct responses to the open-ended questions.

The scoring rubrics for the five problems, together with a generalized rubric, compose Part III of the report. The scheme for scoring responses to each problem consists of a paragraph statement of the requirements of an adequate response, followed by the criteria for scoring students' responses from zero (blank, "don't know") to six. For "inadequate" responses 1 or 2 points are given, 3 or 4 points are awarded to "satisfactory" responses, and 5 or 6 points to responses that show "demonstrated competence." Students' papers representing the upper two scoring categories (3 or 4 and 5 or 6) are attached to the scoring rubric for each problem. Part IV contains 20 examples of students' work and nine additional open-ended problems.

Future Plans

The committee recommended that open-ended questions become a regular part of the mathematics portion of the *Survey of Academic Skills: Grade 12*, starting with the 1988–89 administration of the test. As the other grade level tests are revised, similar kinds of questions will likely be included at those grade levels as well.

Summary of Students' Performance on the Open-ended Questions

Of the approximately 500 papers reviewed for each problem, the following are the percentages of students whose answers showed "demonstrated competence," were "satisfactory," or were "inadequate." Percentages of students giving no response also appear.

. . . summary of students' performance

Problem	Demonstrated competence (in percent)	Satisfactory (in percent)	Inadequate (in percent)	No response (in percent)
A	15	24	59	2
B	14	21	58	7
C	20	12	65	3
D	15	27	52	6
E	9	41	32	18

Students' performance would improve with more writing and oral work.

The committee members surmised that the inadequate responses of a large number of students occurred primarily because students are not accustomed to writing about mathematics. It is likely that students' performance on open-ended questions would vastly improve if students were given opportunities to describe their thought processes orally or in writing while solving problems. Problems that involve reasoning, recognizing patterns or relationships, analyzing situations using knowledge of mathematics, and examining operational relationships would be particularly valuable. Although the committee made recommendations regarding the implications for teaching related to students' misconceptions, committee members emphasized that classroom teachers are in the best position to assess what needs to be done to help their students improve.

Part II

Discussion of Results

Part II contains a discussion of the findings from the students' responses to problems A, B, C, D, and E. The committee's general expectations are described. Strengths and weaknesses in students' responses are examined; included are sections on students' misconceptions and teaching implications. Finally, the results of the students' responses and the instructional implications are summarized.

Problem A

Imagine you are talking to a student in your class on the telephone and want the student to draw some figures. The other student cannot see the figures. Write a set of directions so that the other student can draw the figures exactly as shown below.

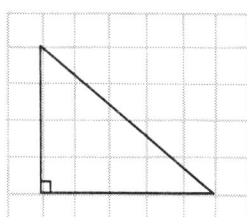
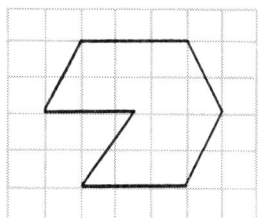

General Expectations

Ability to communicate mathematical ideas with clarity is an important component of mathematical power as emphasized in the California *Mathematics Framework*. Good communication, both verbal and written, indicates understanding. Understanding of a problem and ability to think are prerequisites to successful problem solving.

Problem A assessed the skills of communicating about geometric shapes. It requires students to use effective terminology to describe

Problem A requires effective use of terminology.

the necessary features, in correct steps, to reproduce the given geometric shapes. Responses revealed how well students formulated and communicated mathematical ideas. No single solution or method was correct. An effective solution would result in the precise reproduction of the figures. The use of the word *exact* in the problem implied that the student's written directions would preserve the scale and orientation of the figures. It was also hoped that the instructions would be concise, mathematically elegant, and easy to follow.

Strengths and Weaknesses in Students' Responses

Students' strong responses generally followed one of three approaches: use of geometric terminology, coordinate geometry, or an algorithm. Examples 1, 2, 3, and 4 illustrate students' actual responses using one of these approaches successfully:

Example 1.

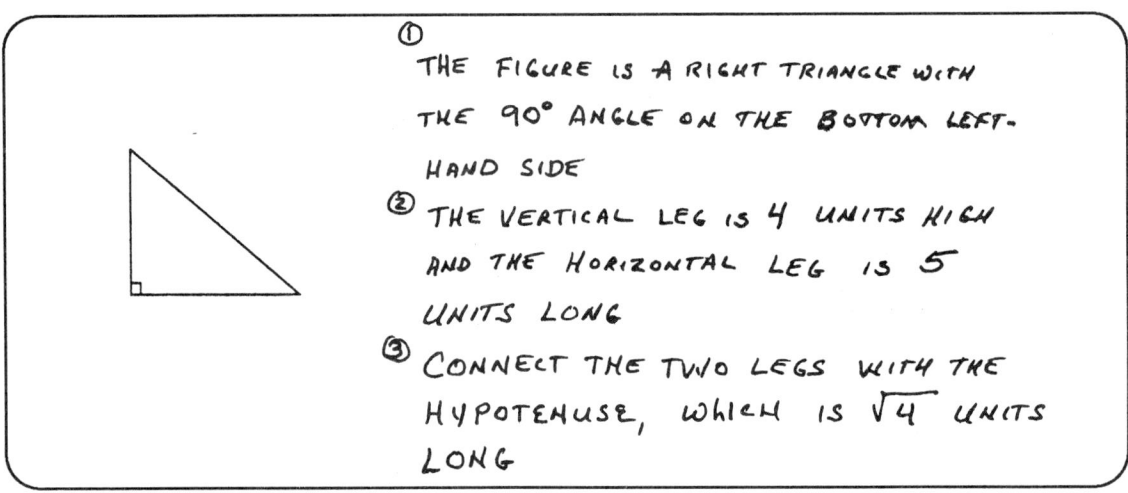

① THE FIGURE IS A RIGHT TRIANGLE WITH THE 90° ANGLE ON THE BOTTOM LEFT-HAND SIDE
② THE VERTICAL LEG IS 4 UNITS HIGH AND THE HORIZONTAL LEG IS 5 UNITS LONG
③ CONNECT THE TWO LEGS WITH THE HYPOTENUSE, WHICH IS $\sqrt{41}$ UNITS LONG

Example 2.

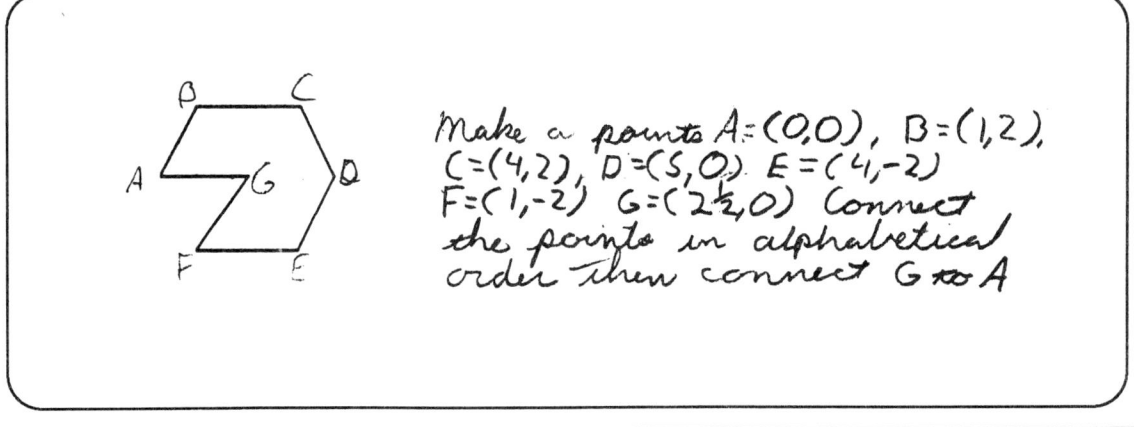

Make a points $A=(0,0)$, $B=(1,2)$, $C=(4,2)$, $D=(5,0)$ $E=(4,-2)$ $F=(1,-2)$ $G=(2\frac{1}{2},0)$ Connect the points in alphabetical order then connect G to A

...problem A students' responses

Example 3.

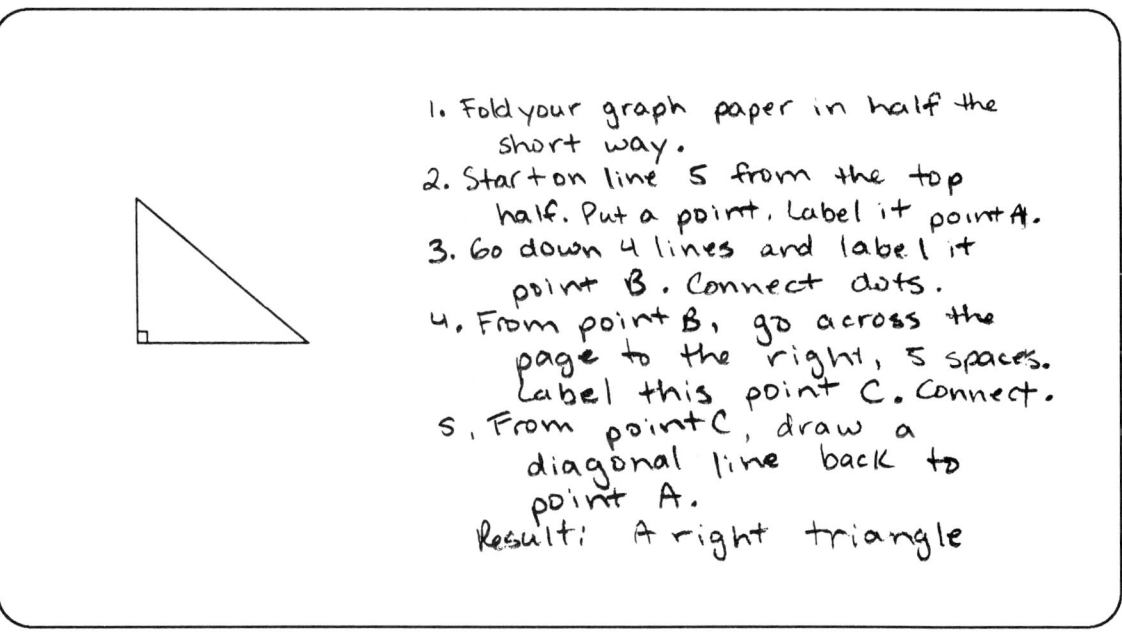

1. Fold your graph paper in half the short way.
2. Start on line 5 from the top half. Put a point. Label it point A.
3. Go down 4 lines and label it point B. Connect dots.
4. From point B, go across the page to the right, 5 spaces. Label this point C. Connect.
5. From point C, draw a diagonal line back to point A.

Result: A right triangle

Example 4.

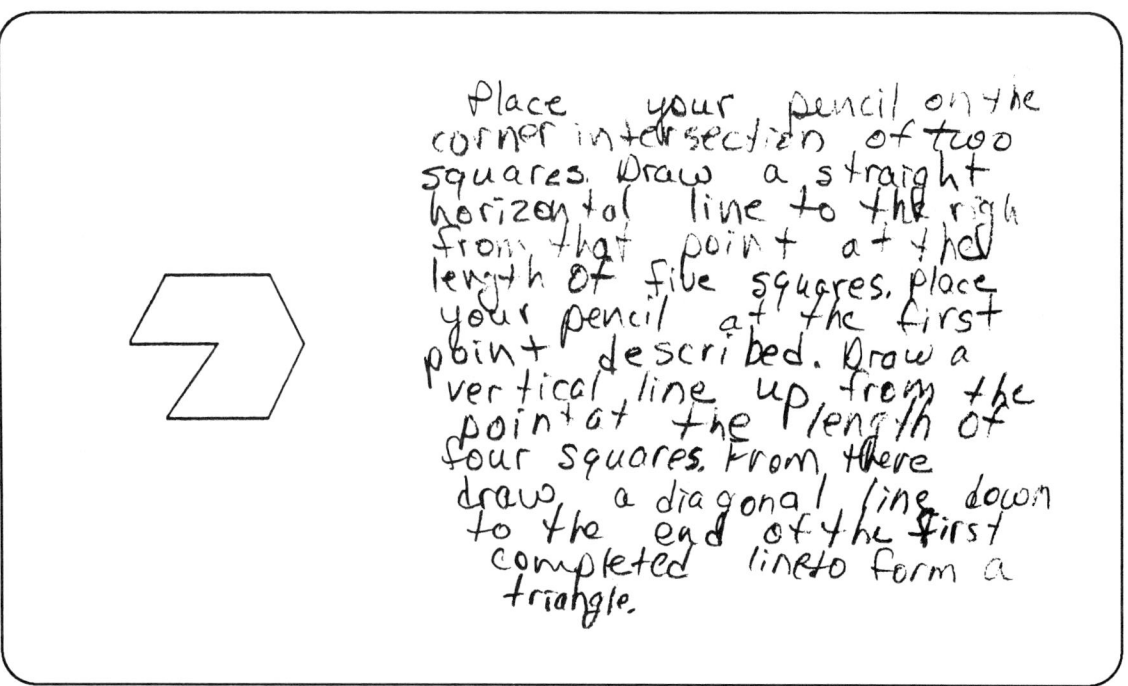

Place your pencil on the corner intersection of two squares. Draw a straight horizontal line to the right from that point at the length of five squares. Place your pencil at the first point described. Draw a vertical line up from the point at the length of four squares. From there draw a diagonal line down to the end of the first completed line to form a triangle.

problem A students' responses

Example 1 shows that the student effectively used the knowledge of geometric terminology (right triangle, vertical/horizontal leg, and hypotenuse). In Example 2 the student used knowledge of coordinate geometry to provide directions for reproducing the figure. In examples 3 and 4, the students took a dot-to-dot, or an algorithmic approach, to describe the figure. In Example 4, however, the student's wording is somewhat cumbersome and excessive. Group discussions and editing of writing in mathematics should help students to achieve more concise and elegant expression of ideas.

For most students, limited use of concepts marred the explanation.

The most serious difficulty for students was inadequate use of concepts to help communicate the instructions. **For a vast majority of students, limited use of concepts got in the way of clear explanation.** Some other obstacles included misuse of algebraic terms; tangled, cumbersome descriptions; and failure to note details such as scale, length of lines, or orientation of the figure. Examples 5, 6, and 7 show some of these misconceptions and related implications for classroom instruction.

Example 5.

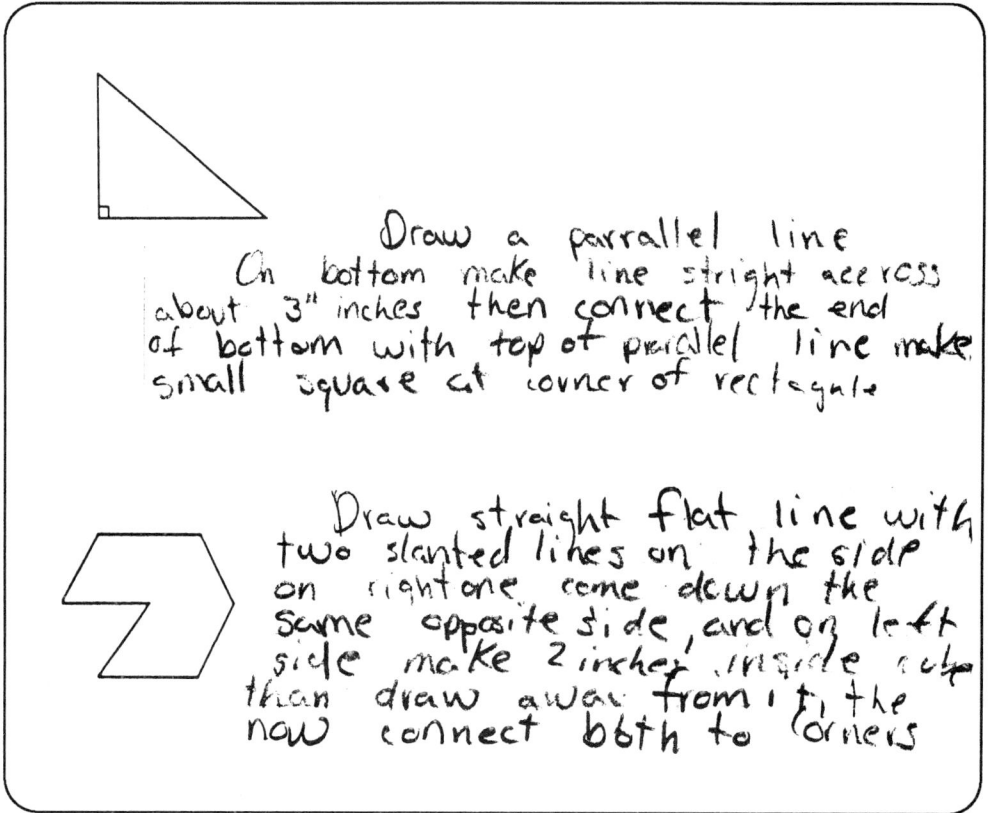

Misconception:
Students attempted to use inappropriate mathematical terms.

Teaching Implications:
Students need experiences explaining and defining ideas using mathematical terminology.

Example 6.

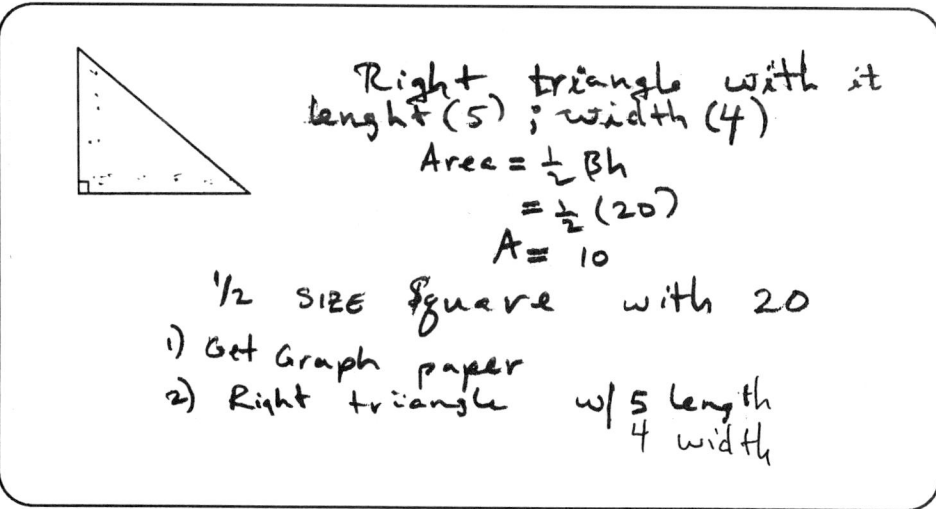

Misconception:
Students applied inappropriate algebraic formulas.

Teaching Implications:
In their eagerness to solve a problem, students often develop solutions before they know what it is they are solving for. The teacher's role is to guide students to read the problem, assess the situation, and figure out what is required.

... problem A summary of results

Example 7.

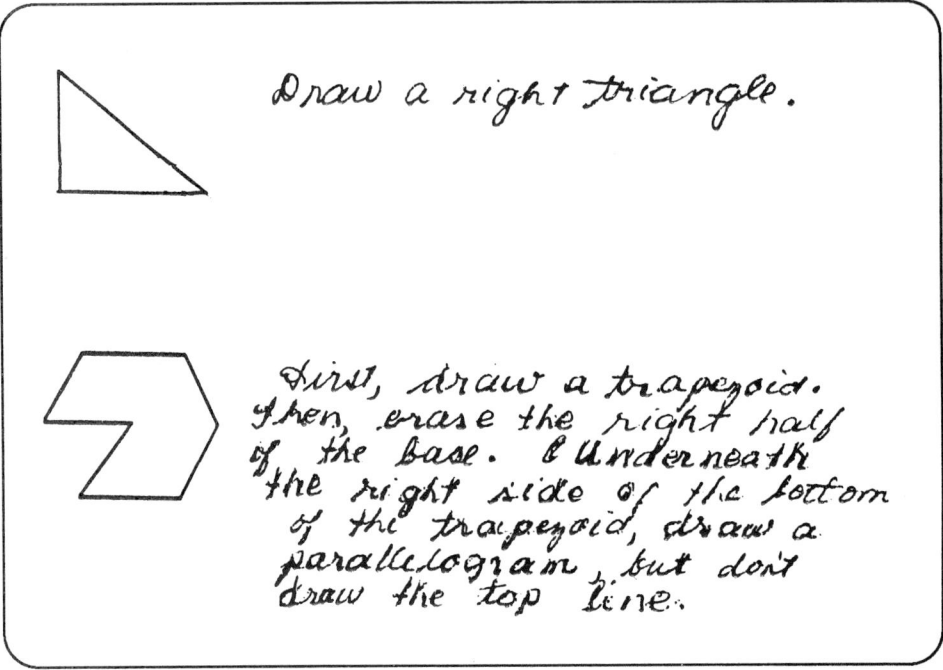

Misconception:
Students failed to consider scale, length of lines, use of graph paper, or orientation of the figure on the page.

Teaching Implications:
Activities in which students give and follow each other's directions will give students insights into achieving accuracy, completeness, and clarity of assumptions.

Giving and following directions lead to insights.

Summary of Results and Instructional Implications

Of the approximately 500 papers scored, fewer than 15 percent showed a solid response. Overall, the reviewers felt that most students at the twelfth grade level were not proficient at this sort of communication. **The reviewers, most of whom were classroom teachers, commented that very few students seem to have had enough experience to be able to write explanations, give directions, or use mathematical terminology in writing explanations.**

Few students are able to use mathematical terminology in writing explanations.

The committee members suggested that classroom activities include opportunities for students to write instructions to others for completing mathematical tasks. Students can share this writing with each other and discuss ways in which they can communicate effectively.

...problem B general expectations

Problem B

Look at these plane figures, some of which are not drawn to scale. Investigate what might be wrong (if anything) with the given information. Briefly write your findings and justify your ideas on the basis of geometric principles.

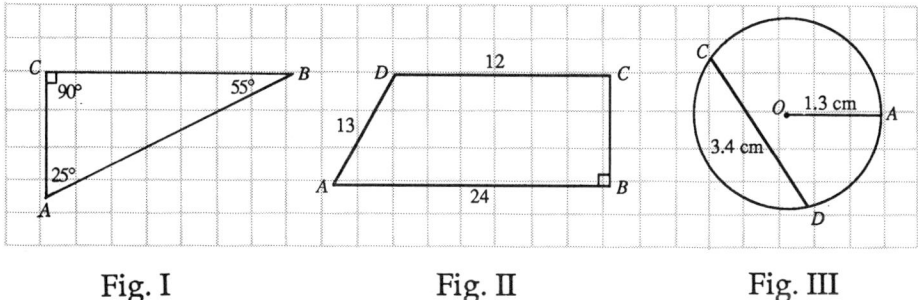

Fig. I   Fig. II   Fig. III

General Expectations

The National Council of Teachers of Mathematics' *Curriculum and Evaluation Standards for School Mathematics* (1989) states that:

> Making conjectures, gathering evidence, and building an argument to support such notions are fundamental to doing mathematics. In fact, a demonstration of good reasoning should be rewarded even more than students' ability to find correct answers.[1]

In Problem B, students were asked to examine three geometric figures to assess their understanding of the relationships between parts of geometric figures and the measures of those parts. For each of the three figures, students were required to make some assertions and justify whether or not the figures were valid, on the basis of geometric principles.

In Problem B, students were asked to make and justify some assertions.

To give a correct response in Figure I, the student would have to indicate that the figure was invalid for any of these reasons:

- No triangle could be formed having the given angle measures since the sum of the measures of the angles of a triangle is 180 degrees.

- No right triangle could be formed having the given angle measures since the sum of the measures of the acute angles of a right triangle is 90 degrees.

---

[1] *Curriculum and Evaluation Standards for School Mathematics.* Reston, Va.: National Council of Teachers of Mathematics, 1989, p. 6.

... problem B general expectations

- Some related theorem or property made the information given false.

Any one or all of the above responses were acceptable, with no one assertion being preferred.

A correct response regarding Figure II required students to recognize that it was possible for a quadrilateral having sides with the given measures to exist. Students should realize that the figure was a trapezoid, even though it was not drawn to scale. They could use the square angle ABC or the coordinate grid to emphasize that AB and CD were parallel.

In Figure III it was expected that students would recognize that either the measure of the radius (and hence the diameter) or the measure of the chord CD was incorrect.

Strengths and Weaknesses in Students' Responses

Students giving strong responses used precise language and logic.

A feature of strong responses was the students' ability to use precise language to identify which figures were valid or invalid, citing geometric principles (examples 8, 9, and 10). The students provided logical and concise justifications. An extremely small number of students questioned whether or not point O was indeed the center of the given circle, and that observation was also valid.

Example 8.

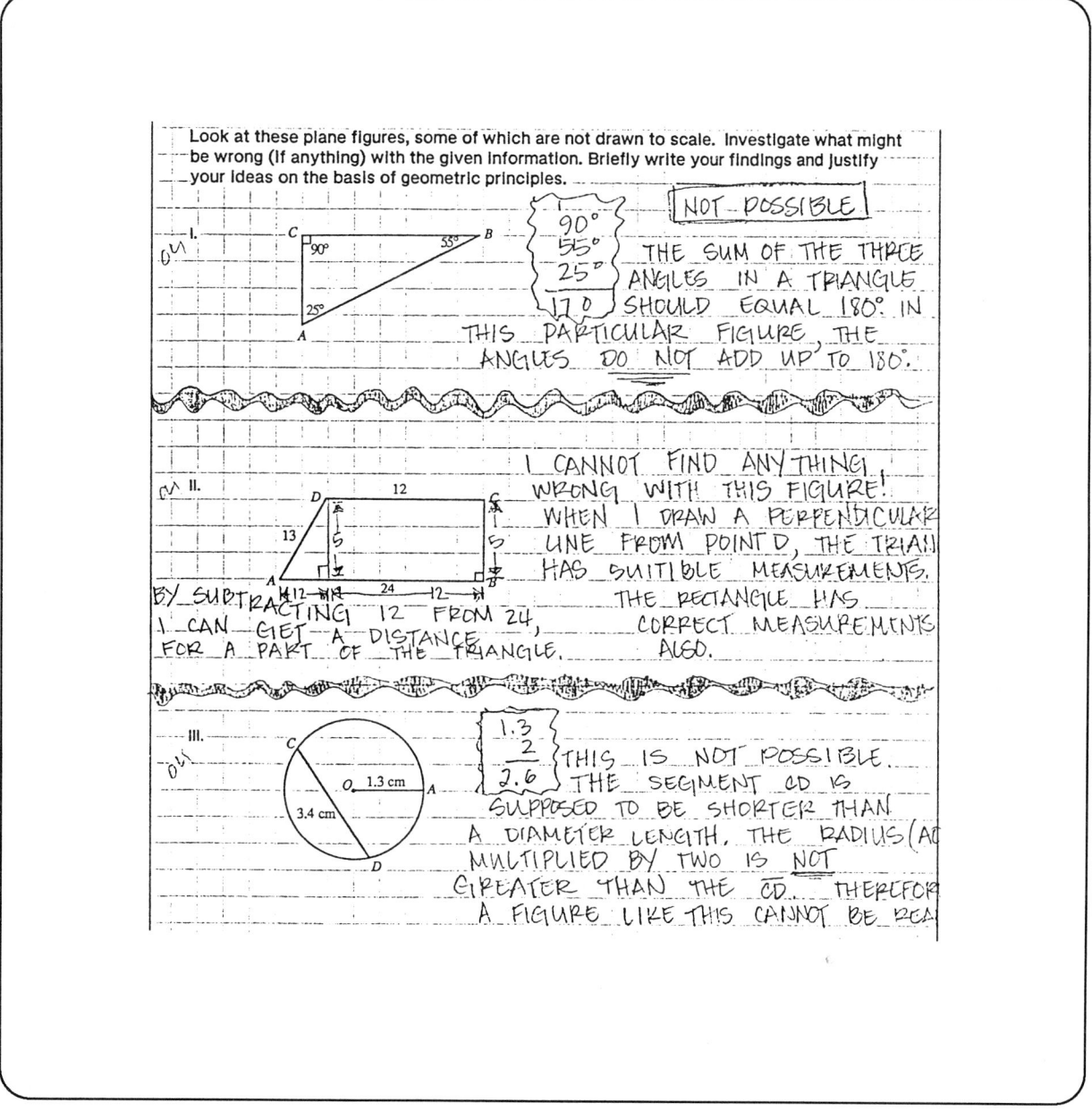

... problem B students' responses

Example 9.

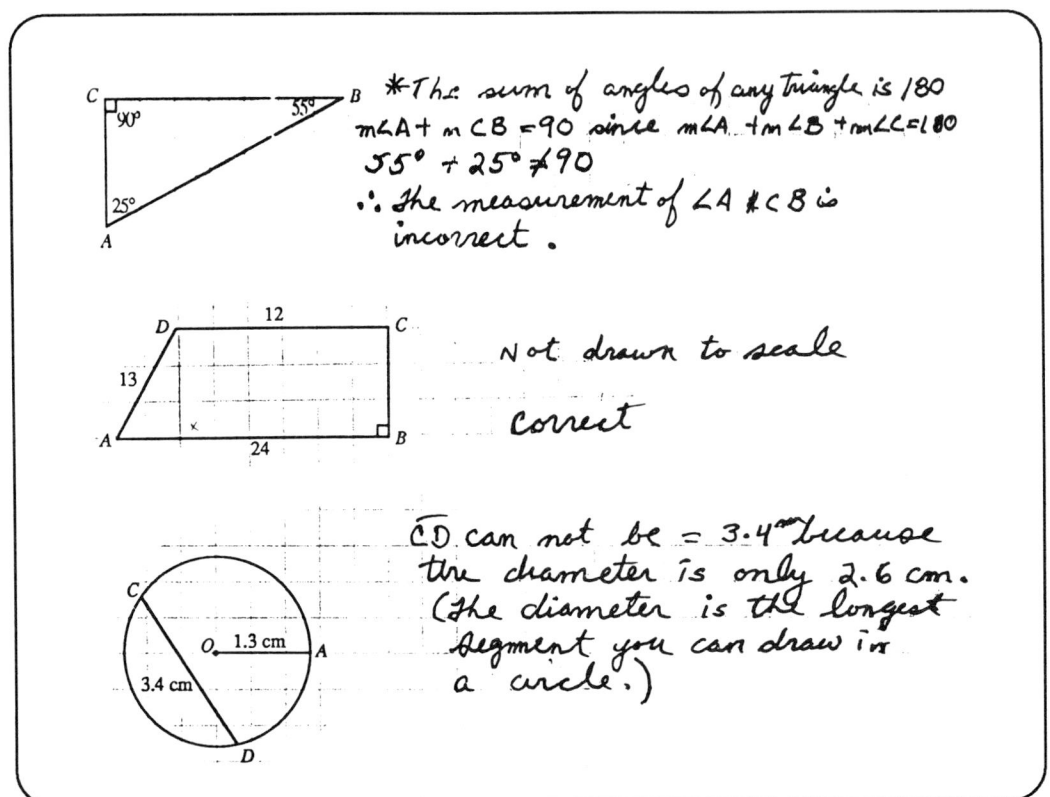

* The sum of angles of any triangle is 180
m∠A + m∠B = 90 since m∠A + m∠B + m∠C = 180
55° + 25° ≠ 90
∴ the measurement of ∠A & ∠B is incorrect.

Not drawn to scale

correct

CD can not be = 3.4" because the diameter is only 2.6 cm. (The diameter is the longest segment you can draw in a circle.)

Example 10.

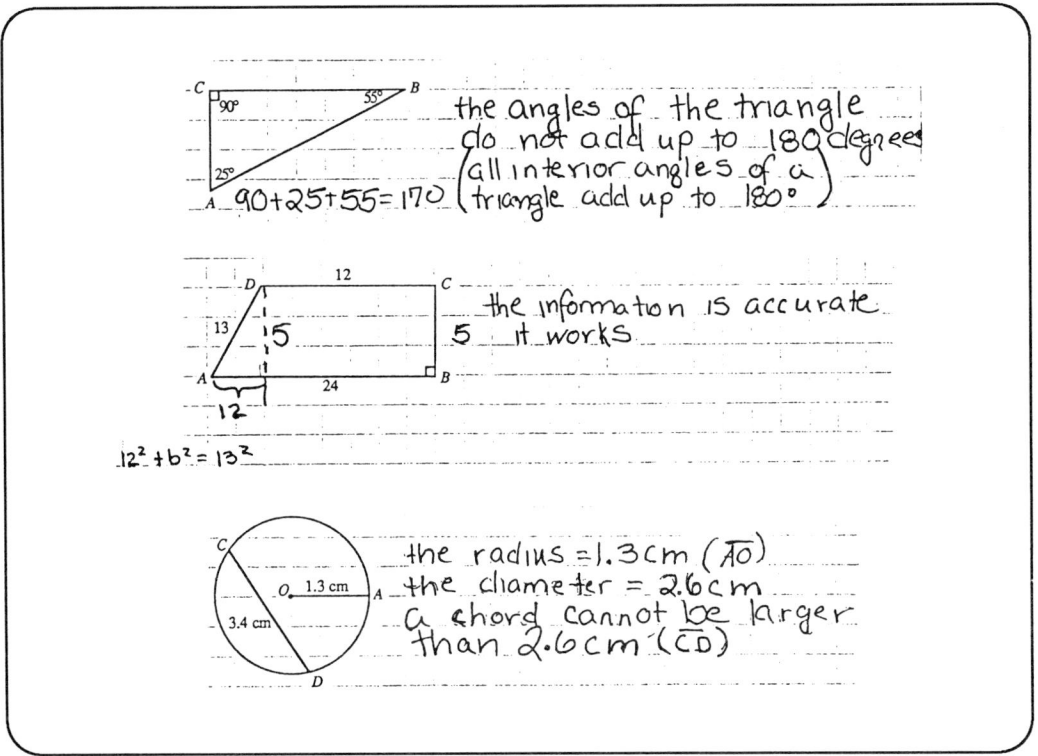

the angles of the triangle do not add up to 180 degrees (all interior angles of a triangle add up to 180°)
$A\ 90 + 25 + 55 = 170$

$12^2 + b^2 = 13^2$

the information is accurate
it works

the radius = 1.3 cm ($\overline{AO}$)
the diameter = 2.6 cm
a chord cannot be larger than 2.6 cm ($\overline{CD}$)

...problem B students' responses

A typical weakness in students' responses was the inappropriate use of geometric principles or imprecise use of language. Students wrote such phrases as, "A triangle is 180° not 170°." In Figure III they said that chord *CD* was a "ray," a "tangent," or a "diameter." Other difficulties are illustrated by excerpts from students' papers (see examples 11 through 17).

Students typically misuse geometric principles and use language imprecisely.

Some common misconceptions were identified by the committee members, who then made the suggestions appearing in "Teaching Implications" to assist in classroom instruction.

Example 11.

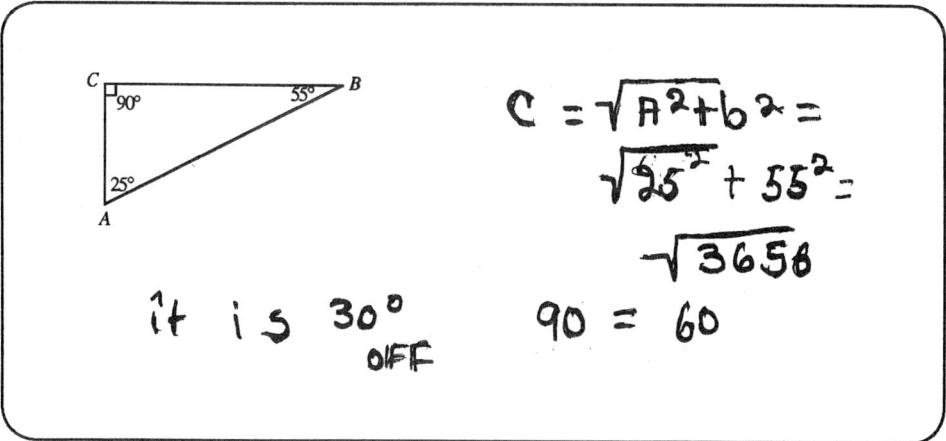

Misconception:
Students often resorted to applying inappropriate formulas to generate a sequence of steps, whether correct or not. For example, students erroneously used the measures of angles as lengths of sides and applied the Pythagorean theorem.

Teaching Implications
Students might be asked to justify their reasoning orally or in writing. Discussion problems should help students rely more on understanding the effective use of mathematics rather than mechanically applying memorized formulas and procedures. Students generally lack a concrete basis for the geometric relations they learn.

Discussion problems help students rely more on understanding mathematics.

...problem B students' responses

Example 12.

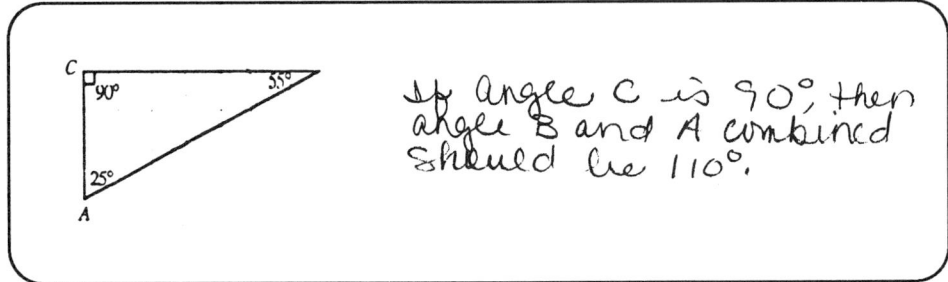

Misconception:
Students thought that the sum of the interior angles of a triangle is something other than 180 degrees.

Geometric figures need to be taught through the use of a variety of concrete methods.

Teaching Implications:
Students' knowledge of triangles and other geometric figures needs to be taught through the use of a variety of concrete methods; for example, scissors and paper folding (cut off the angles and lay them on a straight line).

Example 13.

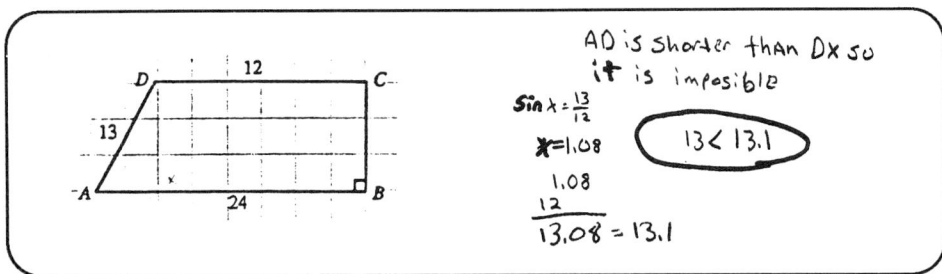

Misconception:
Students used a trigonometric or other unduly advanced approach *incorrectly* to arrive at, or bluff, a solution.

Ability to judge the reasonableness of a solution is very important.

Teaching Implications:
Students need to approach any problem with a multitude of strategies. Ability to judge the reasonableness of a solution is very important. More experience with a variety of methods is needed.

Example 14.

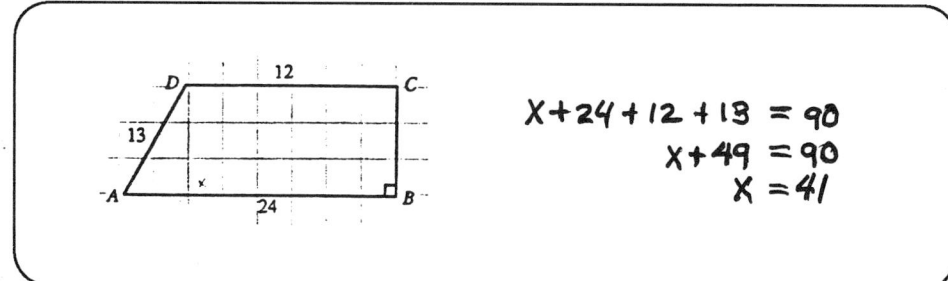

Misconception:
Students bring in the "magic" number 90 when referring to angles, but they used it this time for a perimeter.

Teaching Implications:
Students need to understand the differences between area, perimeter, and angle measurement, using investigations with manipulatives and holding discussions in cooperative learning groups.

Students need to understand the differences between area, perimeter, and angle measurement.

Example 15.

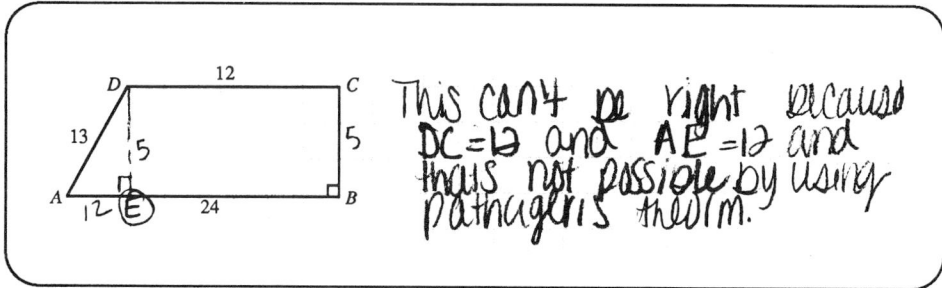

Misconception:
This student derived a correct relationship through the use of geometrical knowledge; but having made false assumptions based on the drawing, he failed to draw the correct conclusion.

Teaching Implications:
Students must learn never to go by what something looks like. Instead, they should read the directions and stick to the point of the problem. Students must stay focused on their goal and practice summarizing the results of their calculations. Emphasizing the goal of each problem should assist these students in their solutions.

Students must learn never to rely on a geometric figure's appearance.

... problem B students' responses

Example 16.

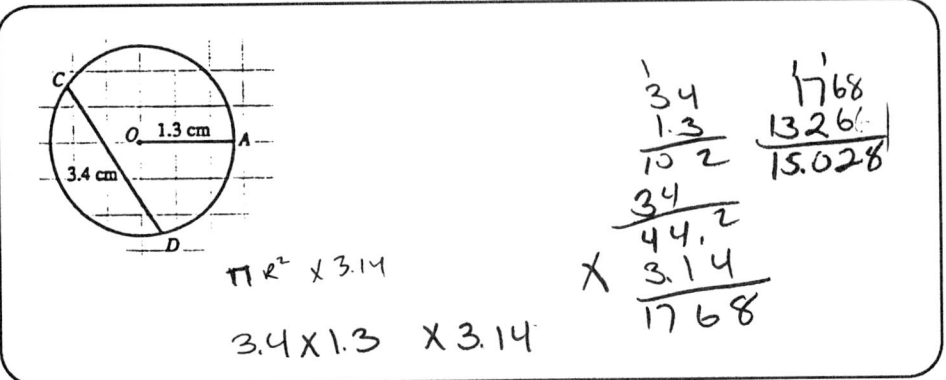

Misconception:
Students thought that inserting available numbers into the formula for the area of a circle would generate the correct result.

Students should not use formulas in isolation.

Teaching Implications:
Awareness of what makes sense in a given problem must be emphasized. Students should not be taught to use formulas in isolation.

Example 17.

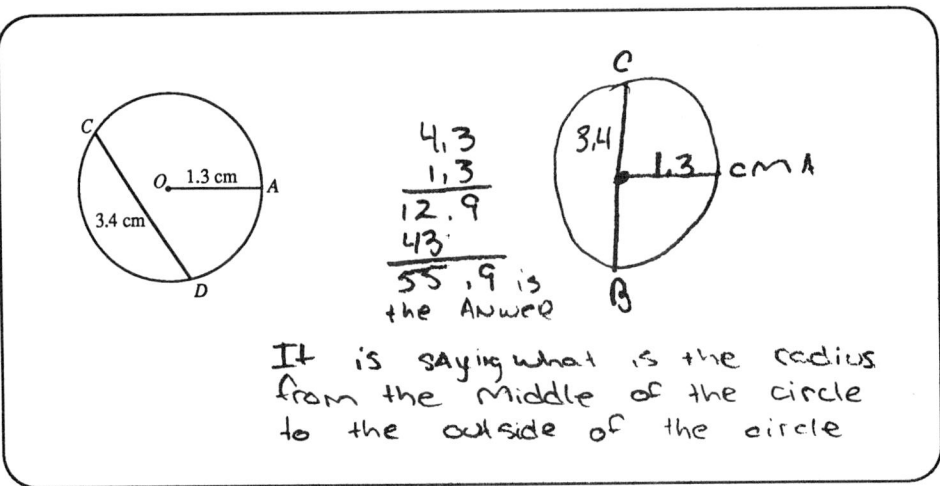

Misconception:
Students bluffed, giving the appearance of trying out something sensible.

Students need to understand rather than guess at answers.

Teaching Implications:
Students often resort to senseless manipulation of data in order to try to get an answer. They need more experience communicating their understanding rather than guessing at answers.

Summary of Results and Instructional Implications

Of the approximately 500 papers scored by the committee, fewer than 14 percent provided a response to Problem B that was more than adequate. For the most part, the justifications written in Problem B were slightly better than the "directions" written in Problem A; however, the quality was still only marginally acceptable overall. Although almost all students responded to one or more of these geometric problems, the directions to justify were often ignored, or students' justifications minimally supported their assertions.

Many students gave minimal justification, if any, for their assertions.

The committee suggests that students be given more learning time with geometric relationships that can be measured and those that must be supported by theorems. The ability to communicate these relationships effectively is crucial to many professions.

Students need opportunities to start at a concrete level and develop formulas themselves. Beyond that, they need to work on situations where many formulas might be used, and they have to choose the one that is helpful.

Problem C

James knows that half of the students from his school are accepted at the public university nearby. Also, half are accepted at the local private college. James thinks that this adds up to 100 percent, so he will surely be accepted at one or the other institution. Explain why James may be wrong. If possible, use a diagram in your explanation.

General Expectations

An important aspect of mathematical power is the need to use logic and diagrams to make sense of a situation and to communicate this reasoning. Diagrams are an effective analytical and communications tool. Problem C assesses the ability to detect erroneous reasoning and requires a clear and mathematically correct explanation of the faulty reasoning. Specifically, the problem demands a recognition that acceptances from the different institutions are not mutually exclusive. The students' responses should focus on the faulty reasoning involving James's assumption of nonoverlapping sets. A variety of diagrams or explanations could be used to help clarify the situation; no particular one was preferred.

Problem C assesses the ability to detect and explain faulty reasoning.

... problem C students' responses

Strengths and Weaknesses in Students' Responses

Of the students who succeeded in understanding and solving this problem, all were able to make a statement to the effect that some students may be accepted at both schools.

This type of response was judged to be adequate in showing a grasp of the problem, but good responses included more complete explanations with examples and/or counterexamples and diagrams that clarified the reasoning. In fact, the variety of diagramming techniques was very exciting and included Venn diagrams, picture diagrams, keyed lists, comic strips, and pie graphs or charts. The diagrams used by those who were successful in solving this problem indicate that at least some students have had opportunities to create and analyze such models in their mathematics instruction. Examples 18 through 22 illustrate good responses from students.

Types of figures included Venn diagrams, pictures, comic strips, and pie graphs or charts.

Example 18.

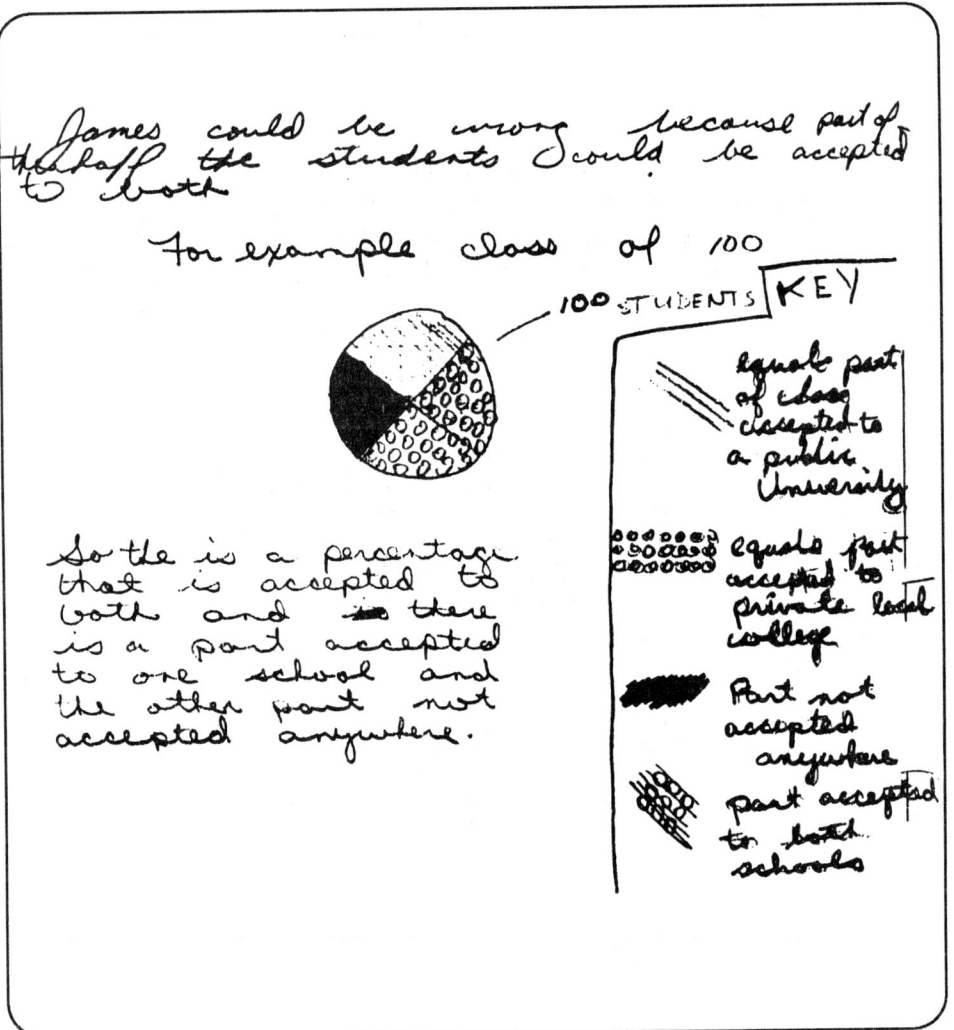

Example 19.

Example 20.

...*problem C students' responses*

Example 21.

James THINKS this adds up to 100%, but there may be students who are accepted to both institutions, thus leaving James out in the cold.

For example, say there are 100 people at his school. Half aet accepted at Public U., the other half at Private U.

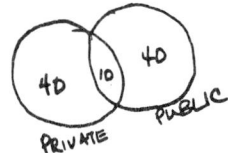

50 were accepted at Private U. 50 were accepted at Public U. But this only accounts for 90% of the students. Jim could be in the other 10%, thus not getting accepted

Example 22.

Half of the students are accepted at the public university. Also, half are accepted at the local private college. The latter statement does not state specifically of what the half are. The half that are accepted at the local private college can also be all, partially, or not at all accepted at the public university. For example:

let (Pu) represent the half of the students who are accepted at the public university,

(L) represents the half of the students who are accepted at the local private college

There are three possible situations:

A) (Pu) (L)   B) (Pu⊗L)   C) (Pu/L)
   ↓   ↓   ↓
which is true   Partially   all of them are
in Jame's theory overlaped   accepted at both schools

Therefore in cases B & C James is wrong. We can then conclude that James may be wrong in the end result.

... problem C students' responses

Students whose responses were inadequate digressed from the problem, focusing on extraneous factors such as grades or graduation requirements. Others simply were unable to make sense of the problem and gave inappropriate answers or made misleading assumptions. The committee members identified some of the common misconceptions and made the suggestions appearing in "Teaching Implications" to assist in classroom instruction.

Example 23.

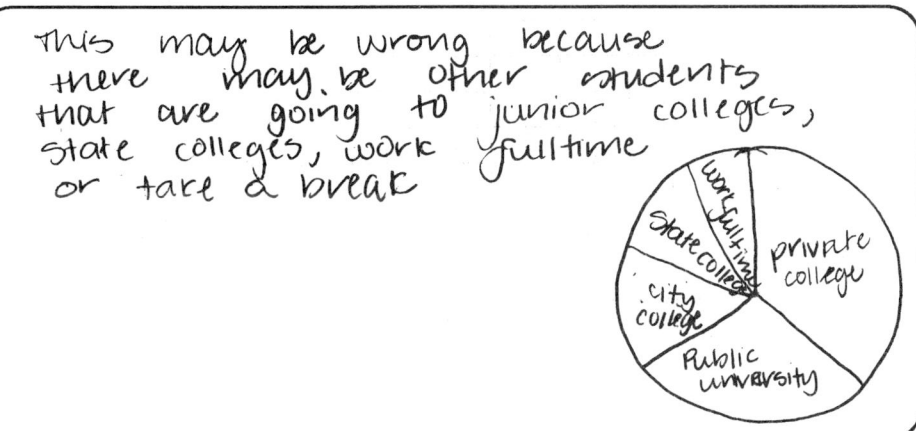

Example 24.

> Thats wrong because everyone doesnt go to college. I think its
>
> 15% doesnt go
> 45 That goes to local college
> 40 That goes to private college

Misconception:
Students questioned the hypotheses of the problem, made inappropriate assumptions, or did not correct James's reasoning.

Teaching Implications:
Students should be asked to distinguish among the given conditions of a situation, hidden assumptions, and unjustified assumptions. Students should articulate their reasoning in evaluating their own and their peers' reasoning. In addition to having students do formal proofs, using theorems, teachers should provide frequent group discussion, writing, and drawing of diagrams.

Students must distinguish between given conditions and unjustified assumptions.

... problem C students' responses

Example 25.

$$\frac{1}{2} \times \frac{1}{2} = 1$$
$$\frac{1}{2}x = \frac{1}{2}$$
$$-\frac{1}{2} \quad \frac{-1}{2}$$
$$x = \frac{1}{2}$$

	private	$\frac{1}{2}$	$\frac{1}{2}x$
	public	$\frac{1}{2}$	$\frac{1}{2}x$

$$2\frac{1}{2}x + \frac{1}{2}x = 1 \cdot 2$$
$$x \cdot \frac{1}{2}x = 2$$
$$1\frac{1}{2}x = 2$$
$$-1\frac{1}{2} \quad 1\frac{1}{2}$$
$$x = \frac{1}{2}$$

Students often resorted to meaningless symbol manipulation.

Misconception:
Students often resorted to meaningless manipulation of symbols when confronted with a new problem situation. This student unsuccessfully attempted to produce an equation to represent the situation.

Developing strategies should be emphasized.

Teaching Implications:
The emphasis in the classroom should be on discussing and developing appropriate strategies rather than on simply finding an answer.

Example 26.

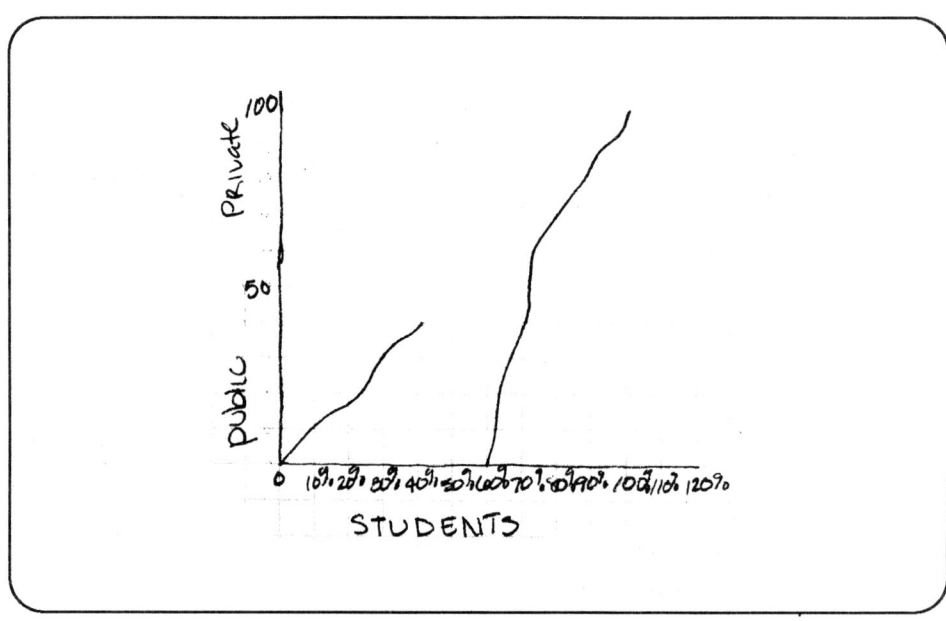

26

Example 27.

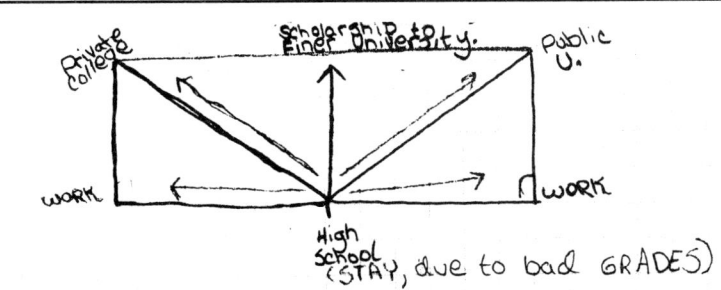

3 Hypothesis

1. STUDENTS MAY RECEIVE scholarships Elsewhere
2. GRADUATES MAY WANT TO WORK
3. STUDENTS MAY FLUNK OUT IN HIGH SCHOOL

Misconception:
Students were unable to provide an appropriate diagram to enhance their explanations.

Teaching Implications:
Students need more opportunities to read, interpret, and create charts, tables, diagrams, and graphs. **They should be able to abstract mathematical information from a situation and develop a model that represents the information.**

Students should be able to abstract information from a situation and develop a model.

Example 28.

If 175 students apply, and ½ are accepted to the public university and ½ are accepted to the local private college.

½ of 175 is 87.   (175)

87 go to the university $87 \times 2 = 174$
87 go to the college
leaving one student out, which can be James

...problem C summary of results

Misconception:
Students used an invalid assumption that the number of students was odd in attempting to prove that James's inference was incorrect.

Teaching Implications:
Students should be taught the use of tools such as Venn diagrams in order to identify false inferences in situations involving logic.

Students should be taught to use such tools as Venn diagrams.

Summary of Results and Instructional Implications

Of the approximately 500 papers scored, only 20 percent of the responses showed that students were able to explain, with or without the help of diagrams, that an overlap can exist between the groups admitted to the college and the university. Approximately 25 percent of the students in the sample digressed from the point of the problem. Another 40 percent were unable to interpret the situation sensibly and gave inappropriate answers.

In summary, the sample of responses to this problem showed a great need for an increase in experiences for *all* secondary students with diagrams and graphs, nonroutine problems, and recognition and interpretation of faulty reasoning.

Students need to distinguish between important and extraneous information.

Although students and teachers should become accustomed to accepting and encouraging a variety of responses, we recommend that teachers help students *focus* on what the problem asks for. Students should identify important information and avoid using added considerations that are not relevant to solving the problem.

... problem D general expectations

Problem D

Consider the following problems.

A. Marla has a job after school. Last week she worked 2 hours and earned $10.50. How much did she earn per hour?

B. This week Marla worked 2 hours and earned $10.50 per hour. How much did she earn this week?

C. Marla worked two jobs. She earned $5.25 on the first and $10.50 on the second. How much did she earn altogether?

   1. Which two problems are most similar and why?

   2. Which two problems are most dissimilar and why?

General Expectations

One important problem-solving strategy is to relate a given problem to a simpler or similar problem that can be solved or that has already been solved. To use this technique effectively, one must be able to identify those parts of the problems that are similar and to justify why the given information, relationships, or outcomes are indeed similar and which parts are dissimilar.

In Problem D it was expected that students would choose some criterion or strategy that had mathematical significance and look for patterns of similarities or differences against that criterion or strategy. In fact, the question was written so that any pair of the three statements could be treated as most similar or dissimilar depending on the criteria chosen.

Students needed to choose a significant criterion as a basis for comparison.

Strengths and Weaknesses in Students' Responses

Students whose responses were strong identified the mathematical criteria and other criteria on which they based their judgments and showed how their choices reflected these criteria. In addition, they indicated why the nonselected problem in each case failed to meet the criteria. However, none of the students took the problem beyond what specifically was asked for in order to describe how different criteria would produce different answers.

The declining strength evident in responses of students between examples 29 and 32 parallels the variation in their ability to think mathematically and express themselves in comparisons and contrasts involving complex mathematical criteria.

Many students have difficulty in making mathematical comparisons.

... *problem D students' responses*

Example 29.

> The two problems that are most similar are problem A and problem B. Problem C does not fit into the same category as the first two. The first problem requires one to divide the total hours by the total earned to figure out an hourly wage and the second problem asked its reader to multiply the two numbers to find a weekly wage. These problems are both dealing with hourly wages and both need to be figured using multiplication since division is just the inverse function of multiplication. However problem C deals with addition.
>
> The two problems that are most dissimilar are problem A and problem C. They are really related in no way. Problem B and C are related because they both ask for an overall total and problems A and B are related for the reasons discussed above. On the other hand, finding an hourly wage by division and finding a total earning by simple addition are totally different. Therefore the two problems that are most dissimilar are problems A and C.

In this example the student described both similarities and differences to justify the pairs selected.

Example 29 is a particularly strong response. A clear thinker and writer, the student compared and contrasted problems on several mathematically relevant features: hourly wage as a rate; multiplication and division as inverse operations, in contrast to addition; and overall total contrasted with rate. In describing both similarities and differences among problems, the student explained why the third problem in each case was not selected.

Example 30.

> Problems A and B are most similar, because in both Marla worked 2 hours on her job. In the first (A) she earned $10.50, and you only need to divide by two to figure her earnings each hour ($5.25). And in B she earns $10.50 per hour, and you only need to multiply by two to calculate her earnings this week ($21.00)
>
> Problems A and C are most dissimilar, because in A Marla worked two hours on the same job and you divide her earnings per hour (see above) while in C Marla worked two jobs and you add the earnings together ($15.75).

The student in Example 30 used a less important mathematical criterion than that given for Example 29 ("worked two hours") as the initial criterion for similarity between problems A and B. Yet, this student also strongly implied hourly wage rate as the major criterion for similarity. The student used two criteria for dissimilarity between problems A and C: two hours versus two jobs and division versus addition. However, the student did not acknowledge that the same rationale could be applied to dissimilarities between problems B and C. In neither case, similarity or dissimilarity of the problems, did the student mention reasons for excluding the nonselected problem.

In this example the student applied the chosen criteria inconsistently.

Example 31.

> A & B because you have to multiply or divide a given amount by an hourly wage

...problem D students' responses

The explanation in this example is too brief and awkward to convey the concept of rate.

The student in Example 31 recognized the major criterion for similarity between problems A and B, the concept of hourly wage rate. But the student's explanation is too brief and awkward to convey clearly the concept of rate or to ensure that the student himself understands it well enough to use it.

Example 32.

> 1. Which two problems are most similar and why?
>
> A+B   Because Marla has one (1) job in both, worked the same number of hours.
>
> 2. Which two problems are most dissimilar and why?
>
> A+C   Because Marla has different jobs, different wages.

Finally, the student in Example 32 mentioned two minor points of similarity ("one job, same number of hours" for each problem) between problems A and B, but he did not refer to rate or hourly wage as the major criterion for similarity. The student's oversimplified criterion of "different jobs, different wages" for the dissimilarity between A and C did not provide justification for the nonselection of B.

Teaching Implications:

Examples 29 through 32 illustrate the range of students' abilities regarding this kind of problem. The results show that students need more opportunities to classify problems by multiple criteria. They need practice in justifying their choice of criteria for classification, demonstrating that the criteria are appropriate to the comparison or contrast. In particular, students need more work looking for *mathematical concepts* as a basis for classification rather than identifying only isolated numbers that are similar or different.

Students need practice in justifying their classification criteria.

Inadequate responses focused on characteristics not relevant to the problem's context.

Inadequate responses to Problem D focused on such characteristics as the numbers in the problem, or Marla's name appearing first in the sentence, without regard to the context of the situation being described. Those students who gave inadequate responses were not classifying similarity and differences among problems A, B, and C as complex situations. Instead, they were discussing only one or two surface similarities or differences in the numbers or mathematical terms stated in the problems. In some cases, they inferred information that was not given.

... problem D students' responses

Example 33.

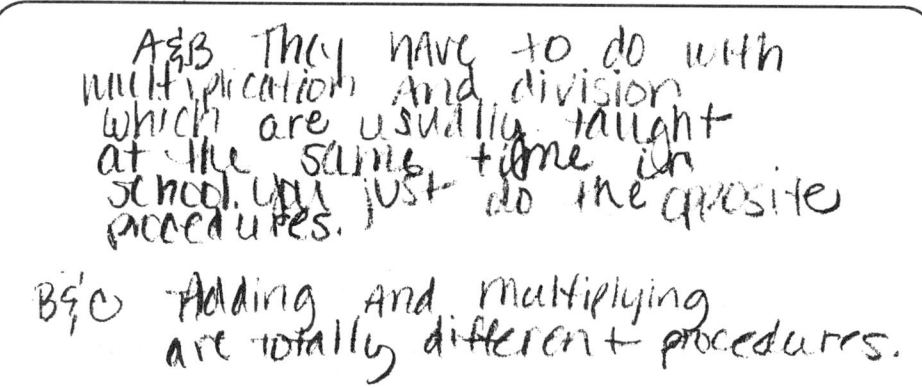
> A&B They have to do with multiplication and division which are usually taught at the same time in school. You just do the opposite procedures.
>
> B&C Adding and multiplying are totally different procedures.

Misconception:
In classifying the similarities or dissimilarities among problems, students focused only on the criterion of what operation is used to find the solution. The student in Example 33 classified problems A and B as similar because of the inverse operations of multiplication and division taught concurrently in school. Students who classify problems on vague and simplistic criteria are likely to make false inferences about what problems require.

Using vague or simplistic criteria often leads to false inferences.

Teaching Implications:
Classification of problems only by what operations are used seems to reflect textbook organization of problem sets. (All problems in a set are solved using the same operations—only the numbers are changed.) This arrangement seems to lead to student questions such as, "Do we add or multiply to solve these problems?" Focusing on one technique per problem set apparently produces the desire to use those operations in all problems in a set, regardless of the information that is pertinent in the problem.

Example 34.

> 1. Which two problems are most similar and why?
> A,B -Because she work the same hours and made same money.
>
> 2. Which two problems are most dissimilar and why?
> C,A She didn't make the same

33

...problem D students' responses

Example 35.

> 1. Which two problems are most similar and why? A & C
> Because it askes how much did they earn but only has different wages.

Example 36.

> Ⓐ $5.25
> 2⟌$10.50
>
> Ⓑ $10.50
> × 2
> $21.00
>
> Ⓒ $10.50
> + 5.25
> $15.75
>
> The problems A & C are most similar because she earned the same amount per hour.

Misconception:
In examples 34, 35, and 36, students failed to recognize some of the relationships involved in each problem. This failure usually involved misinterpretation of the information requested.

Teaching Implications:
Students jump to conclusions based on the use of similar numbers in the opening sentences of the problems. Students need increased opportunities to identify the information given in the problem, its purpose, and its use in solving the problem.

Students need more opportunities to identify and use given information.

Example 37.

> A 10.50 = 2x
>   5.25 = x
>
> B 10.50
>   × 2
> $21.00
>
> C 10.50
>   + 5.25
>   15.75
>
> Problems A and B are the most similar because Marla worked 2 hrs in both weeks.

Example 38.

> Problems A and C are most dissimilar because she earned $10.50 in A but earned $5.25 for her first job in problem C.

Misconception:
In examples 37 and 38, students focused on a single number as a basis for declaring problems similar or dissimilar.

Teaching Implications:
Making a variety of comparisons in problem situations is a useful technique for resolving those situations. Identifying multiple criteria for claiming similarity or dissimilarity can be helpful in developing an understanding of problems.

Summary of Results and Instructional Implications

Of the approximately 500 papers scored for problem D, fewer than 20 percent of the responses were more than adequate. Students who wrote good responses compared problems in a variety of ways, using mathematical rather than incidental criteria.

The responses as a whole indicated to the committee that many students are aware of some of the characteristics by which problems can be classified. Furthermore, some students can develop effective arguments. In general, students looked for some kind of criteria for establishing similarity and difference, although the criteria chosen may have been surface features rather than mathematical features of the problem. A few of the better responses included an explanation of why the criteria chosen were appropriate for classifying these types of problems.

A majority of students simply classified the problems by the basic operation to be used in solving the problem, without giving any additional explanation. Many students chose to compare these problems on the basis of either surface characteristics or irrelevant assumptions, indicating a lack of experience with situations requiring them to analyze characteristics that different problems have in common.

Approximately 27 percent of the students chose to describe the differences because of the ways in which the problems were stated. Another 15 percent of the students attempted to justify their choices with reasons that were based on superficial features; for example, comparing numbers, wording, or more general aspects of the situation. Students who focused on superficial or irrelevant characteristics had probably not had enough experience in classifying problems according to mathematical concepts.

A majority of students simply classified problems by the arithmetic operations used to solve them.

Superficial responses indicate a lack of experience in classification.

...problem E general expectations

The committee recommends that teachers give students more opportunities to classify problems by multiple criteria in order to encourage students to look for *mathematical* differences or similarities rather than incidental differences; that is, differences that are not significant within the context of a mathematical situation.

Problem E

The square shown below has sides of length 2 units. Connect the midpoints of the sides of the square, in order, to form an <u>interior</u> square. Repeat the same process to make squares within squares.

(a) Draw the first five <u>interior</u> squares.

(b) Write the sequence of numbers that represent the areas of the first five <u>interior</u> squares.

(c) What rule can be used to find the areas of the nth <u>interior</u> square?

General Expectations

Students had to draw a set of telescoping squares and observe the pattern formed by the sequence of areas.

In Problem E, students had to follow directions to draw a figure showing the telescoping of five interior squares. Then they had to calculate the areas of the interior squares, organize the information so that any pattern present could be observed, and conjecture about a general rule that could govern the situation. Algebra II textbooks frequently include problems similar to this one that challenge students' creativity.

Strengths and Weaknesses in Students' Responses

The students who were able to translate correctly from the verbal description to a geometric figure made drawings that were neat, accurate, and complete, showing the telescoping of the five interior squares. Students who drew the figure correctly and also calculated the areas of the five interior squares generally appeared to use one of three approaches:

- They used the Pythagorean theorem, found the length of a side, and then found the area.

- They counted squares and partial squares on the grid behind the figure.

- They used a "transformations solution" by folding the corners of the larger squares inward to become the size of the next inner square. This procedure was not demonstrated, of course, but some students appeared to have visualized this process and used it in their solution.

Students who conjectured about a general rule for the area of the nth square used either an algebraic expression for the nth term of a sequence or stated a recursion rule. The algebraic formula for using n to find the area of the nth square was given in a variety of forms:

$$A_n = 2^{2-n}, \quad A_n = \frac{4}{2^n}, \quad A_n = \frac{1}{2^{n-2}}, \text{ etc.}$$

The recursion formula was sometimes stated in words ("To find the area of the nth square, divide the area of the previous square by 2") or as a formula:

$$A_1 = 2$$
$$A_n = \frac{A_{n-1}}{2}$$

Examples 39 and 40 illustrate strong responses from students who completed all three steps of the problem: drawing the five telescoped interior squares, computing the sequence of areas, and stating a general rule.

Example 39.

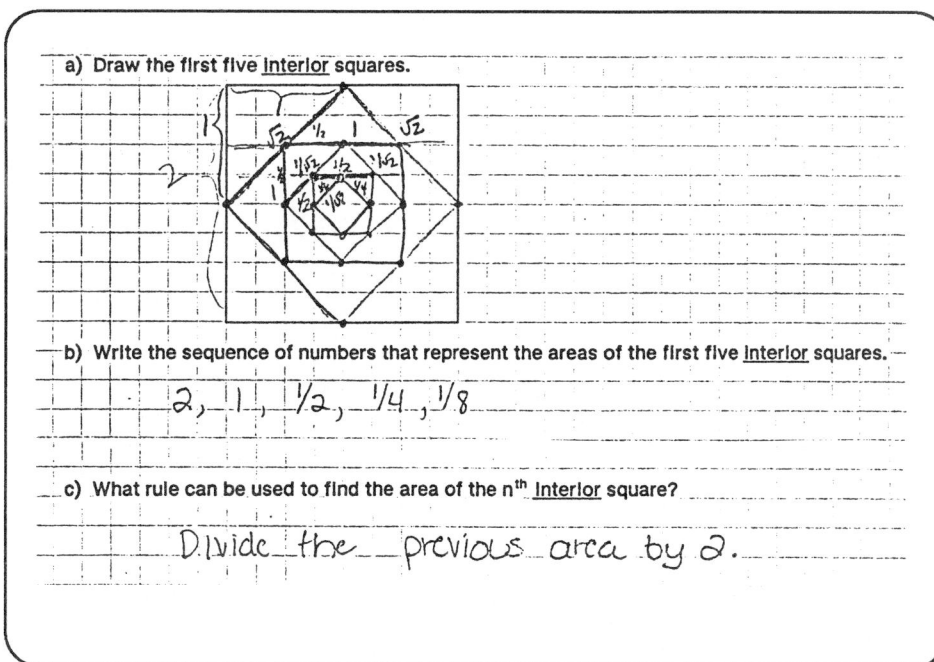

... problem E students' responses

Example 40.

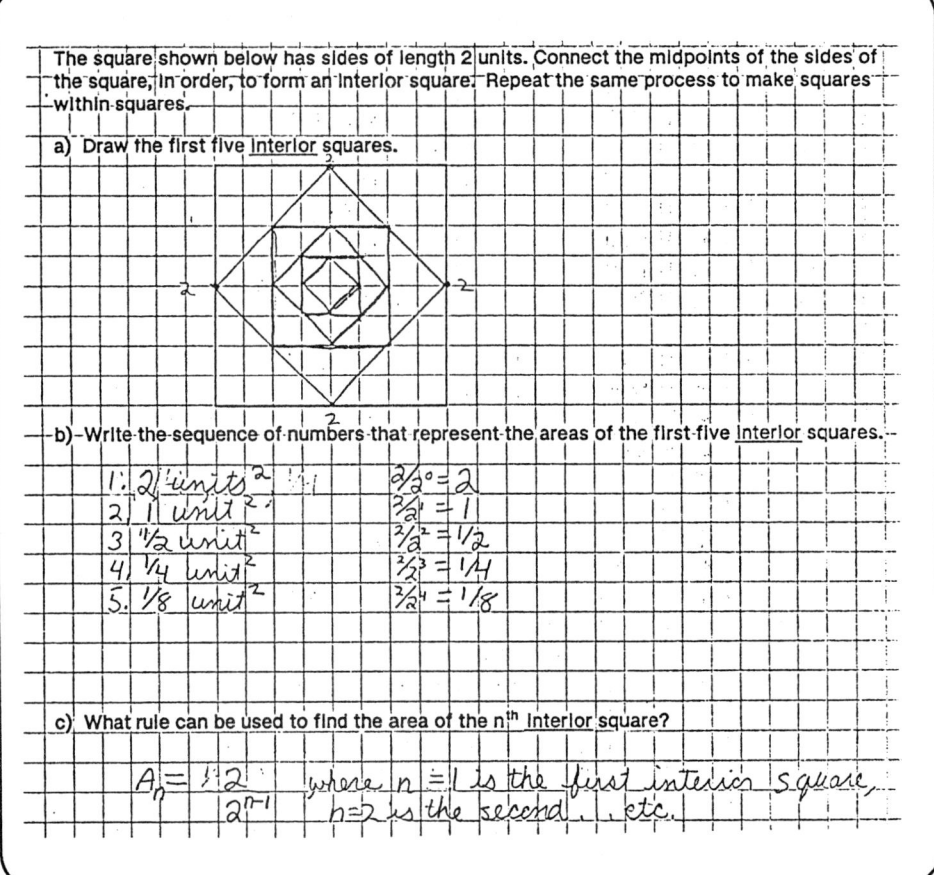

Misconception:

The majority of students were unable to complete step (a) of the problem.

The majority of students were unable to complete successfully step (a) of the problem, "draw the first five interior squares." **One-fifth left the paper entirely blank.** Many others either misunderstood the terms used in the question such as *midpoint, square, interior, connect, five,* and *in order*; or they could not assemble them into a coherent whole so as to translate a set of verbal instructions into an appropriate geometric figure. Example 41 shows three students' attempts:

Example 41.

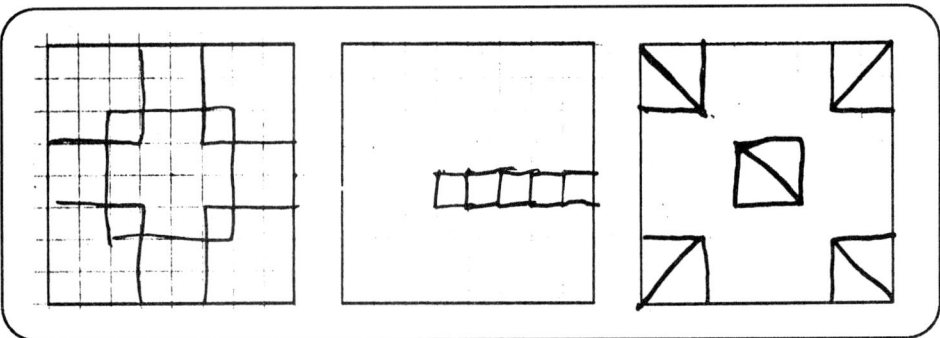

...problem E students' responses

Misconception:
Many students ignored instructions to connect midpoints and simply drew the squares anywhere in the interior of the original square. The most common error was to connect opposite rather than consecutive midpoints. Example 42 portrays the drawings of a number of these students:

Example 42.

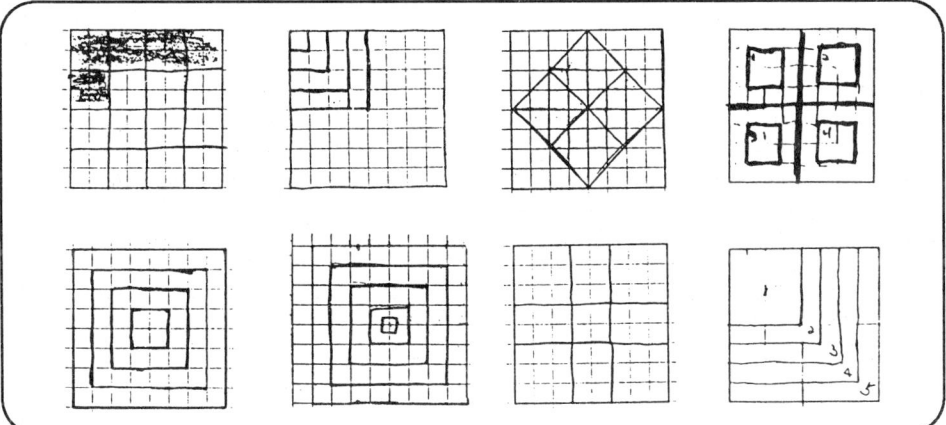

Teaching Implications:
Although students have been given opportunities to translate from verbal situations to equations and arithmetic algorithms, they have not had enough experience in proceeding from verbal instructions to geometric figures. They need practice in using geometrical terms and then putting them together in a coherent whole.

Students have not had enough experience in proceeding from verbal instructions to geometric figures.

Example 43.

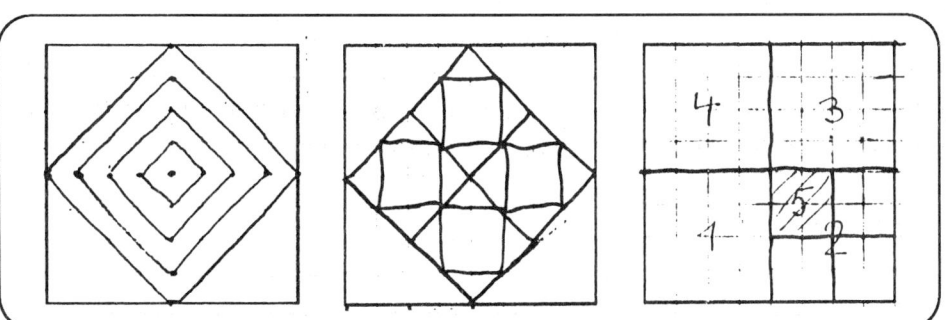

Misconception:
Students took into account only part of the specifications for the figure.

Teaching Implications:
Reading in mathematics is a skill that should be emphasized. Students should list data, select relevant parts, and ensure that all restrictions are applied.

...problem E students' responses

Students who successfully drew the first five interior squares frequently had difficulty with step (b) of the problem, "Write the sequence of numbers that represent the areas of the first five <u>interior</u> squares."

Many students began computing the sequence of areas by assuming the area of the first interior square to be other than two square units. Many were apparently distracted by the grid behind the figure and gave the area of the first interior square to be either 64 or 32. Some students assigned larger dimensions to smaller squares. Example 44 shows erroneous sequences given by eight different students.

Example 44.

Student One	Student Two	Student Three	Student Four	Student Five	Student Six	Student Seven	Student Eight
2.56	1	1	2	3	2	5	n
1.44	2	1	1 1/2	16	4	4	$n+1$
.64	3	1/4	1	26	8	3	$n+2$
.16	4	1/4	1/2	64	11	2	$n+3$
0	5	1/2	0			1	$n+5$

Misconception:
Many students were confused about relative sizes, with dimensions either increasing or remaining the same as the sizes of the squares receded in the interior. **Many of the students who completed steps (a) and (b) of the problem nevertheless were unable to complete step (c), generalizing to a rule that could be used to find the area of the nth <u>interior</u> square.**

Students need to check to see whether answers are reasonable.

Teaching Implications:
Students need to be involved in solving realistic problems with reasonable answers.

Example 45.

... problem E students' responses

Rarely did the students make a chart, a problem-solving strategy that is taught as early as the primary grades; this approach seemed to have been abandoned by these twelfth graders. Those students who did make a chart were generally successful in generalizing to a rule. In Example 45 the student whose response is on the left used a chart to proceed from the number of the square, *n*, to the area of the *n*th square. However, the student whose work is on the right was unsuccessful; but he probably would have been able to find the pattern had he numbered the areas that he computed for the interior squares.

Students who made a chart were generally successful.

Example 46.

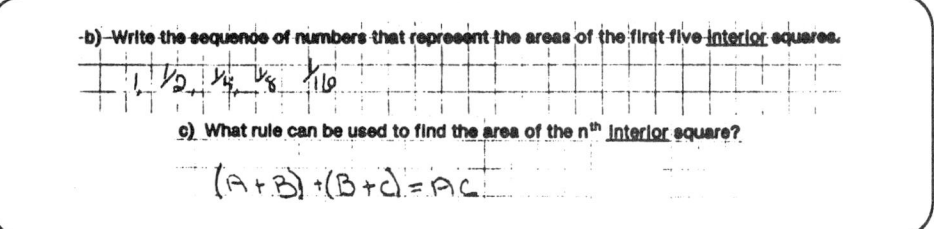

Example 47.

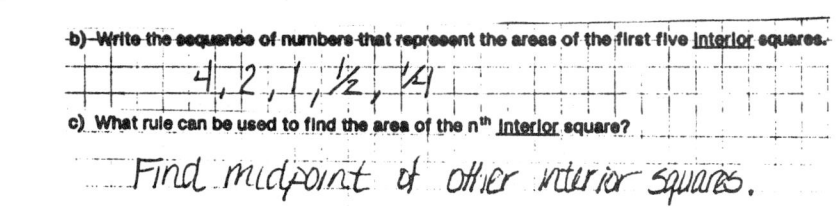

Misconception:
Students failed to observe patterns in the relationship between the number of the square and the area of the square.

Teaching Implications:
Relationships between the elements of a function should be taught on all grade levels and in all levels of classes.

... problem E students' responses

Example 48.

> if area of 1st interior sq = ½ area of original sq
> " " 2nd " " = ½ area of 1st interior sq
> area " 3rd " " = ½ area of 2nd interior sq
> area " 4th " " = ½ area of 3rd " "
> " " 5th " " = ½ area " 4th " "
>
> So 0 = area of original sq.
>
> | Interior squares | | | | |
> |---|---|---|---|---|
> | 1 | 2 | 3 | 4 | 5 |
> | 1/20 | 1/40 | 1/80 | 1/160 | 1/320 |

Misconception:
Some students set up a sequence correctly, but they generalized to an inappropriate rule.

Teaching Implications:
In carefully examining students' work, teachers can ascertain the variety of ways in which students attempt to solve problems. Knowledge of students' thinking processes enables teachers to guide students to make generalizations from appropriate mathematical rules. The examples above suggest that students need repeated instruction on relationships between the elements of a function.

Knowing students' thinking processes can help teachers to guide students toward forming generalizations.

Summary of Results and Instructional Implications

Only a tiny percentage of students completed the problem correctly. More than 20 percent of the students were unable to make any connection between the verbal statement and a figure, leaving the paper entirely blank. Forty-three percent of the students in the sample gave a figure that showed some misconception about the directions.

Of the 37 percent who drew the figure correctly, only about 20 percent (or 7 percent of the entire student sample) were successful in computing the sequence of areas for the five interior squares.

Of the students who found the correct sequence of areas, or a plausible sequence that was partly correct, about 10 percent stated an appropriate rule for their data. Approximately 3 percent of this sample were able to conclude that the area of each successive square was half that of the preceding square. About half of these students were able to write either a general rule or a recursion formula for the sequence.

. . . problem E summary of results

Students' descriptions and diagrams of their work revealed a series of ways they went astray: only 1.5 percent successfully completed the entire problem. Major implications for instruction are fourfold. First, students need experience translating verbal instructions into geometric figures, experimenting until the two correspond. Second, they need practice making charts of the mathematical patterns they discover so that they can generalize to a mathematical rule. Third, they need to highlight the relationships between elements of functions, in this case, between the sequence number of the interior square and its area. Finally, students should go by the information given in the problem and not be misled by the squares on the graph paper. The units of measurement specified in the problem are what is important.

Relationships between elements of functions need to be highlighted.

Part III

Scoring Students' Responses to Open-ended Questions in Mathematics

Part III contains a discussion of the CAP advisory committee's reasons and procedures for developing the scoring rubrics used in the open-ended questions. As a help to persons interested in developing their own rubrics, suggested procedures are given. Scoring rubrics for each of the problems, A through E, and a generalized rubric also appear.

Development of Scoring Rubrics

Open-ended mathematics questions are intended to provide evidence of the student's:

- *Understanding* of mathematics
- *Use* of mathematical knowledge
- *Ability to communicate* about mathematics

Development of scoring rubrics should reflect these aspects. In addition, the *forms* of mathematical thinking required to solve a given problem should be considered. For example, solving an applied measurement question may require a strategy different from that used in attacking a question on probability and statistics. A scoring rubric should describe the strategies students can use to solve a problem as well as the expectations for students' understanding, use, and communication of mathematical concepts.

The CAP advisory committee decided to develop and use individual rubrics to score each of the questions rather than to have a single rubric that would apply for all questions. This need emerged from the concern that a single generalized rubric would mask the particular mathematical outcomes that could be exemplified through a customized rubric. The following method was used to develop the rubrics for problems A through E administered in 1987–88.

First, the committee members looked at each question (without looking at students' papers) and discussed desirable responses for each question. Next, a large sample of papers for each question was read holistically and classified in one of the six categories ranked from 1 to 6, 1 being the lowest and 6 the highest rank. The committee members then described the characteristics of papers falling into each of the six categories. These descriptions were again discussed by committee members to clarify criteria for papers falling into each category. This process was refined during several committee meetings.

The committee also developed a generalized rubric that could be applied to all the questions, the purpose of which was to establish consistency across questions and over a span of years. The committee members strongly believe that the generalized rubric should not be used by itself for scoring; however, this rubric can be a helpful guide to develop specific rubrics for open-ended questions.

The committee members also discussed the scores (1 through 6) in relation to competency in mathematics. The following description shows that relationship:

Competency Levels	Rating/Score
Demonstrated Competence	
Exemplary	6
Competent	5
Satisfactory	
Minor flaws	4
Serious flaws	3
Inadequate	
Begins, but not completed	2
Unable to begin	1
(No attempt)	0

...developing your own rubrics

Procedure for Developing Your Own Rubrics

You are welcome to use the open-ended items printed in this report or other items to develop your own rubrics. Here is a suggested procedure:

1. Have your students work the open-ended problem.
2. Have your faculty colleagues in mathematics do the same problem.
3. Discuss the problem as a faculty group and try to sort the students' papers into six groups, with six being the highest rank and one the lowest.
4. Discuss the characteristics of the responses and articulate a rubric for an exemplary rating (six) response.
5. Articulate rubrics for the other categories.
6. Take a second look at the students' papers and, based on your rubrics, regroup them as needed.

1987–88 Individual Scoring Rubrics for Problems A Through E

The following pages give scoring rubrics for problems A through E administered in 1987–88. A generalized rubric is given at the end of these rubrics, followed by ten marked illustrative papers. Although no rubric is provided for the five 1988–89 open-ended questions, ten marked illustrative papers are provided for that year. Teachers are encouraged to develop their own rubrics for these questions. Preliminary rubrics for 1988–89 can be obtained from the CAP office on request. The address is California Assessment Program, California State Department of Education, P.O. Box 944272, Sacramento, CA 94244-2720; telephone (916) 322-2200.

... problem A scoring rubric

Scoring Rubric for Problem A

A correct response to Problem A requires that the student be capable of giving directions to a peer for reproducing two geometric figures; one, a right triangle; the second, a nonstandard figure. Scorers look for coherent, unambiguous descriptions that make effective use of proper mathematical terminology. To obtain the highest score, students must communicate correct lengths and orientation. Coordinate geometry may be used; the students should then give the order in which points are joined.

Demonstrated Competence

For 6 points: The student, using mathematical ideas, effectively gives a coherent description that would result in the reproduction of a correct figure with respect to side length and orientation. If coordinates are used for Part b, the directions for connecting them must be unambiguous. The instructions can be interpreted easily.

For 5 points: The student gives a coherent description, but there is some minor omission.

Satisfactory Response

For 4 points: The student gives a coherent description, but there is some major omission that would result in figures drawn with errors such as incorrect lengths or orientation.

For 3 points: Adequate descriptions using some mathematical terminology are given, but there are some misdirections, such as failure to describe diagonal segments or failure to direct the student receiving the description to connect parts of the diagram.

Inadequate Response

For 2 points: Inadequate descriptions for drawing the figures are given. While the student uses some mathematical terminology, there are serious omissions or misdirections.

For 1 point: The descriptions of each figure show misuse or minimal use of mathematical ideas.

Off Track: The student leaves a blank page or writes: "I don't know."

Remark: Location of the figures on the paper (top, bottom, or middle) was considered to be a minor issue.

. . . problem B scoring rubric

Scoring Rubric for Problem B

The student must detect errors, or lack thereof, in three geometric figures: a triangle whose angle measures do not add up to 180, a trapezoid, and a circle with a chord longer than twice the radius (i.e., longer than the diameter). To obtain the highest score, students must specifically state that there is no error in the second figure, and they must use good reasoning based on geometric principles in identifying the errors in figures I and III.

Demonstrated Competence

For 6 points: Figures I and III are found incorrect, and good explanations are given, with evidence of high-level thinking in the application of geometric principles. A statement for Figure II indicates that the figure is valid.

For 5 points: Both figures I and III are marked as incorrect, and good explanations are given. No findings are given for Figure II.

Satisfactory Response

For 4 points: Either Figure I or Figure III is marked as incorrect, but the student uses a level of thinking in the explanation that is higher than that in an answer awarded 3 points.

For 3 points: Either Figure I or Figure III is marked as incorrect, and an explanation involving geometric principles is given (e.g., the sum of the measures of the angles in a triangle must be 180 degrees; a chord of a circle cannot be longer than the diameter).

Inadequate Response

For 2 points: Only one of the three findings is correct.

For 1 point: The response indicates some thinking relevant to the task, but none of the student's findings is correct.

Off Track: No relevant response is given, or the page is left blank.

Scoring Rubric for Problem C

Students are given an example of a logic problem that involves college acceptance. The student must give a clear and mathematically correct explanation of the faulty reasoning involving the assumption of nonoverlapping sets in the problem. For the highest score, responses must be complete, contain examples and/or counterexamples of overlapping sets, or have elegantly expressed mathematics. A diagram is expected.

Demonstrated Competence

For 6 points: The response is exemplary. It goes beyond the criteria for 5 points. For example, the response may include:

- Example(s) and/or counterexample(s)
- Mathematics expressed elegantly
- An explanation that is complete

For 5 points: The response is correct and the explanation is clear. It may be expressed in words, with a diagram, or both.

Satisfactory Response

For 4 points: The response is generally correct, but the explanation lacks clarity.

For 3 points: The response indicates a *partial* solution (e.g., the same 50 percent are accepted by both colleges); or the response indicates that the student *may* understand the solution but the explanation is incoherent.

Inadequate Response

For 2 points: The response is incorrect, but it shows evidence of mathematical reasoning. A mathematical explanation is developed. However, the explanation does not address the crux of the problem or the essence of the solution. The paper may include a mathematical misconception.

For 1 point: The response is incorrect. It is not a sensible mathematical solution of the problem. The justification may use irrelevant arguments, such as:

- Whether a student is qualified for college
- Where a student attends college
- Whether a student desires to attend college
- Whether a student has applied to college

Off Track: The student leaves a blank page or writes: "I don't know."

...problem D scoring rubric

Scoring Rubric for Problem D

CAUTION: The scorer must recognize that different parts of a student's response may be accorded different scores. In these cases the scorer must assign a score reflecting the average quality of the total response.

Students are asked to identify and describe the most similar and the most dissimilar pairs from a set of three problem situations. They must identify the mathematical criteria—for example, functions, givens, or goals—on which their judgments are based and show how their choices reflect these criteria. For the highest scores, responses showing students' criteria for classifying problems as most similar or most dissimilar must reflect high-level mathematical thinking. The student must observe and give examples of how different criteria would produce different answers. In addition, the student must show why the problem not selected as most similar or most dissimilar fails to meet the criteria for classification.

Demonstrated Competence

For 6 points: The student observes that the answer to the question will vary according to different mathematical dimensions. He or she gives examples of how the answer might vary. The dimensions used might include functions, givens, and goals. If the student chooses to argue that one pair is more similar to or different from another according to a set of criteria, he or she supports the argument by showing why the nonselected pair is inferior according to the dimensions chosen.

For 5 points: The student identifies the dimensions used to establish the degree of similarity or difference, referring to these dimensions in the examples. Some of the dimensions will represent higher-level mathematical thinking. To receive 5 points, the student must support the argument by showing why the nonselected pair is inferior according to the dimensions chosen.

Satisfactory Response

For 4 points: The student identifies the dimensions used to establish the degree of similarity or difference, referring to the example to illustrate the dimensions he or she selects. The dimensions may not represent as high a level of thinking as that of students who receive 5 points. The student who receives 4 points may not refer to as many dimensions as those who receive 5 points. The student will usually fail to support his or her argument by showing why the nonselected pair is inferior according to the dimensions chosen.

For 3 points:	The student uses some of the components that earn 4 points but fails to give evidence of higher-level mathematical thinking. Although the student generally includes more than one dimension to support the argument, the dimensions still tend to be superficial. The argument may contain minor inaccurate statements.

Inadequate Response

For 2 points:	The student does not identify more than one mathematical dimension of similarity or dissimilarity. This dimension tends to be superficial. The argument may contain inaccurate statements.
For 1 point:	The student attempts to answer the questions but makes major errors. At best, one trivial piece of evidence, such as the appearance of the same constants in two of the problems, is given to prove similarity.
Off Track:	The student leaves a blank page or is off topic; no attempt is made to answer the questions.

... problem E scoring rubric

Scoring Rubric for Problem E

Students must follow instructions to draw correctly a sequence of interior squares based on midpoints of sides of previously drawn squares. They must then calculate areas of interior squares and finally generalize to write a rule for the area of the nth interior square. To receive the highest score, students must complete all three parts of the problem correctly. The rule may be a formula equivalent to $1/2^{n-2}$ or it may be recursive, in which case the area of the initial square must be stated.

Demonstrated Competence

For 6 points: Everything is correct, including the picture (five interior squares), the scale, the sequence of areas, and the rule. The rule may be a formula (equivalent to $1/2^{n-2}$) or recursive, equivalent to $A_1 = 2$, and $A_{n+1} = A_n/2$. Note: The rule "1/2 previous area" without the initial area is *not* adequate.

For 5 points: There is a correct drawing and a correct sequence of areas (e.g., 2, 1, 1/2, 1/4, 1/8) but not a rule.
Or, there is a correct drawing, a correct sequence, and a correct rule except for scale.
Or, there is a modified drawing (not trivial), a consistent sequence to scale, and a consistent rule.

Satisfactory Response

For 4 points: There is a correct drawing for Part a; for Part b, a correct sequence of areas except for the scale derived from mislabeling the original square (e.g., 32, 16, 8, 4, 2); Part c is not attempted.
Or, the problem is modified; but it is nontrivial, and a consistent sequence of areas and a rule (Part c) are given. The scale may still be incorrect.

For 3 points: A correct drawing shows five interior squares; no other correct information is presented.
Or, the problem is altered by a modification of the drawing, producing a trivial problem; a correct solution for Part b is given in accord with the modification.

Inadequate Response

For 2 points: The drawing shows the midpoints of the original square or of subsequent squares, but midpoints are not connected in order. There is no other correct information presented.

For 1 point: Some attempt is made at a solution, but no indication is given of an understanding of midpoints.

Off Track: The student leaves a blank page or writes: "I don't know."

Remark: Misinformation in one part does not reduce points earned in other parts.

Generalized Rubric

Demonstrated Competence

Exemplary Response... Rating = 6
Gives a complete response with a clear, coherent, unambiguous, and elegant explanation; includes a clear and simplified diagram; communicates effectively to the identified audience; shows understanding of the open-ended problem's mathematical ideas and processes; identifies all the important elements of the problem; may include examples and counterexamples; presents strong supporting arguments.

Competent Response... Rating = 5
Gives a fairly complete response with reasonably clear explanations; may include an appropriate diagram; communicates effectively to the identified audience; shows understanding of the problem's mathematical ideas and processes; identifies the most important elements of the problems; presents solid supporting arguments.

Satisfactory Response

Minor Flaws But Satisfactory... Rating = 4
Completes the problem satisfactorily, but the explanation may be muddled; argumentation may be incomplete; diagram may be inappropriate or unclear; understands the underlying mathematical ideas; uses mathematical ideas effectively.

Serious Flaws But Nearly Satisfactory... Rating = 3
Begins the problem appropriately but may fail to complete or may omit significant parts of the problem; may fail to show full understanding of mathematical ideas and processes; may make major computational errors; may misuse or fail to use mathematical terms; response may reflect an inappropriate strategy for solving the problem.

Inadequate Response

Begins, But Fails to Complete Problem... Rating = 2
Explanation is not understandable; diagram may be unclear; shows no understanding of the problem situation; may make major computational errors.

Unable to Begin Effectively... Rating = 1
Words do not reflect the problem; drawings misrepresent the problem situation; copies parts of the problem but without attempting a solution; fails to indicate which information is appropriate to problem.

No Attempt... Rating = 0

Part IV

Additional Responses and Problems

Part IV contains 20 scored students' responses: two each for the ten problems given in 1987 and 1988. Scores appear at the top of each page. The report concludes with a set of nine open-ended problems that have not been been tested. Teachers may wish to try some of these problems in class and develop scoring rubrics for them.

Sample Scored 1987 Responses

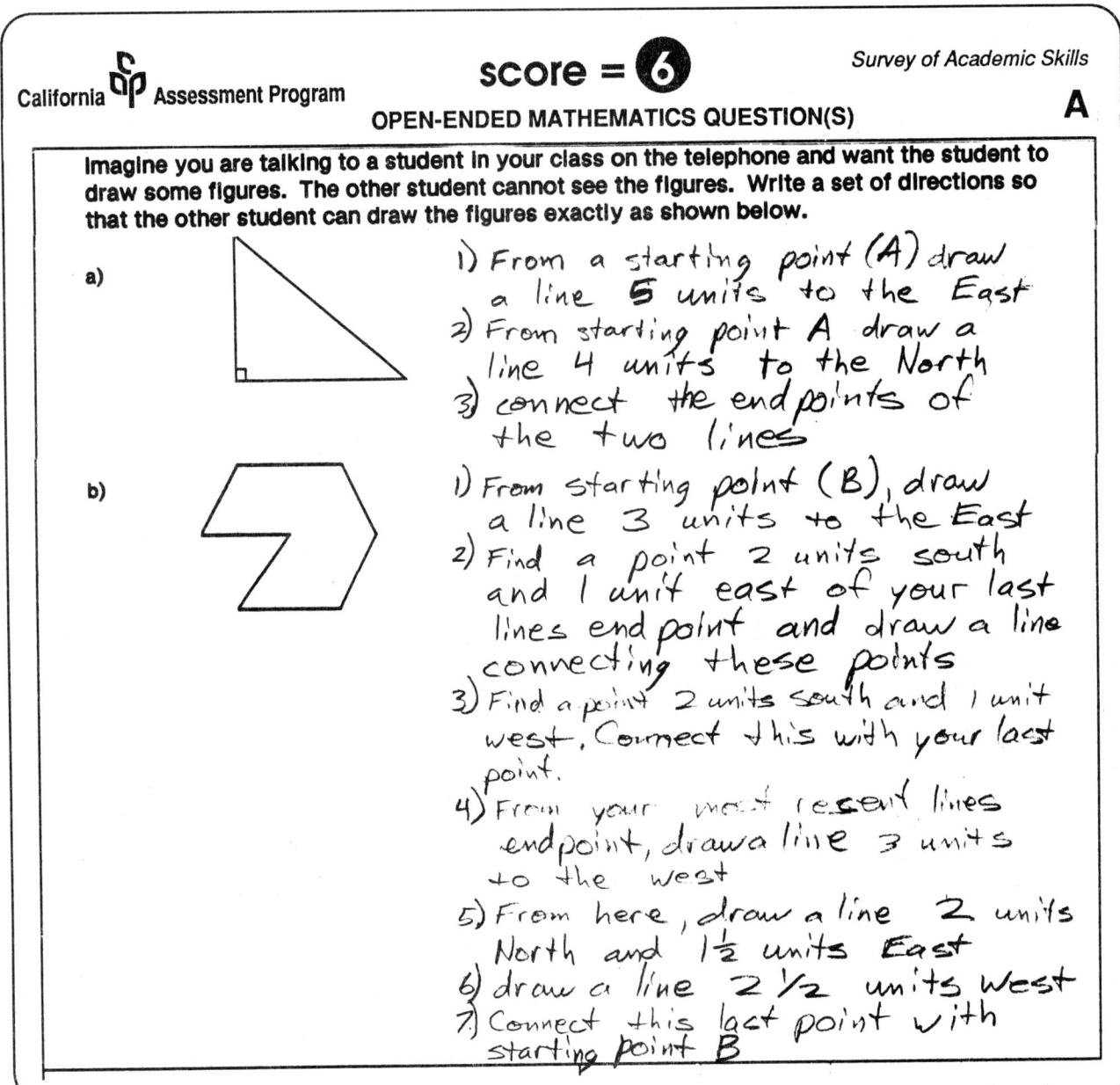

...1987 problem A

California Assessment Program — **score = 4** — *Survey of Academic Skills*

OPEN-ENDED MATHEMATICS QUESTION(S) — **A**

Name_____

Instructions: Use this sheet to answer the questions. Show as much of your work as possible. (In some cases, there may be more than one solution.) Use the reverse side of this sheet if needed.

Imagine you are talking to a student in your class on the telephone and want the student to draw some figures. The other student cannot see the figures. Write a set of directions so that the other student can draw the figures exactly as shown below.

a) Get some graph paper and draw a straight line down 4 squares and a straight line across from where you left off at the bottom 5 lines across. Now from those two points draw a straight line connecting them.

b) For the second one on the bottom half of the same graph paper draw a line across 3 squares. Now draw a line down 2 and across sideways two. Like drawing the roof of a house. Now at the left hand side draw a straight line across to the right through 2½ squares now from that point come out to the left to the first square. Now draw a line across 3 squares, to the right. Now connect the 2 missing dots together. The results are like an Einstein packman facing the left side.

55

...1987 problem B

California Assessment Program — **OPEN-ENDED MATHEMATICS QUESTION(S)**

score = 6

Survey of Academic Skills

B

Name_____

Instructions: Use this sheet to answer the questions. Show as much of your work as possible. (In some cases, there may be more than one solution.) Use the reverse side of this sheet if needed.

Look at these plane figures, some of which are not drawn to scale. Investigate what might be wrong (if anything) with the given information. Briefly write your findings and justify your ideas on the basis of geometric principles.

I.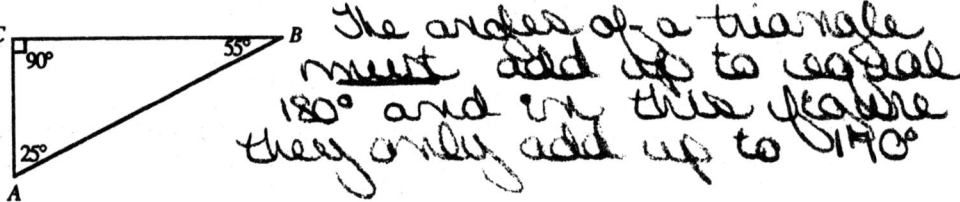

The angles of a triangle must add up to equal 180° and in this figure they only add up to 170°.

II.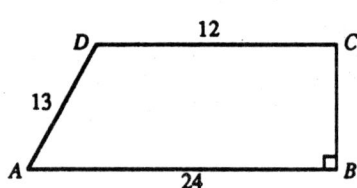

Nothing is wrong.

III.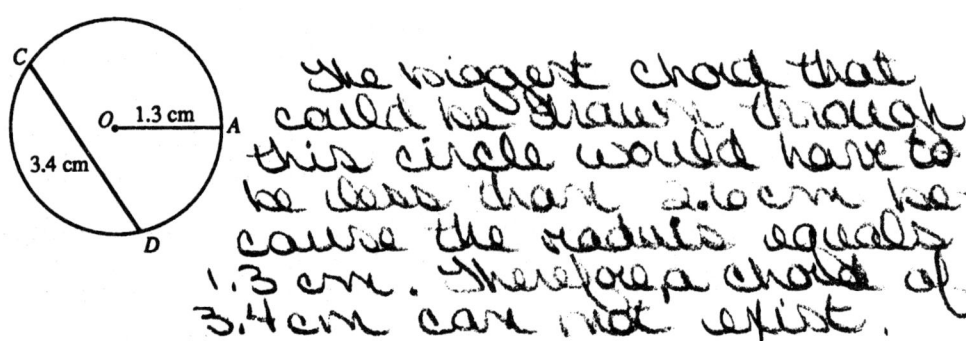

The biggest chord that could be drawn through this circle would have to be less than 2.6 cm because the radius equals 1.3 cm. Therefore a chord of 3.4 cm can not exist.

...1987 problem B

California Assessment Program
score = 5
Survey of Academic Skills
OPEN-ENDED MATHEMATICS QUESTION(S) B

Name_____

Instructions: Use this sheet to answer the questions. Show as much of your work as possible. (In some cases, there may be more than one solution.) Use the reverse side of this sheet if needed.

Look at these plane figures, some of which are not drawn to scale. Investigate what might be wrong (if anything) with the given information. Briefly write your findings and justify your ideas on the basis of geometric principles.

I.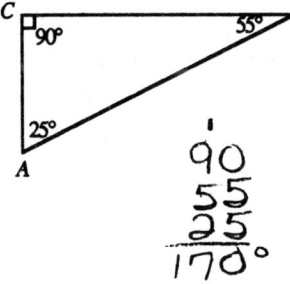

```
 90
 55
 25
----
170°
```

The sum of the three angles should add up to 180° instead of 170°.

II.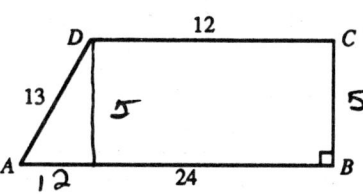

Nothing is wrong except that the figure is not drawn to scale.

$12^2 + x^2 = 13^2$
$144 + x^2 = 169$
-144
$x^2 = 25$ $x = 5$

$\frac{24}{-12}$ / 12

III.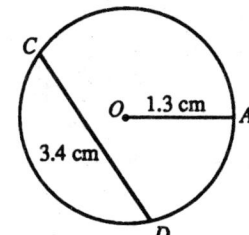

Nothing wrong with the figure

57

...1987 problem C

California Assessment Program — **score = 5** — *Survey of Academic Skills*

OPEN-ENDED MATHEMATICS QUESTION(S) — C

Name_____

Instructions: Use this sheet to answer the questions. Show as much of your work as possible. (In some cases, there may be more than one solution.) Use the reverse side of this sheet if needed.

James knows that half of the students from his school are accepted at the public university nearby. Also, half are accepted at the local private college. James thinks that this adds up to 100%, so he will surely be accepted at one or the other institution. Explain why James may be wrong. If possible, use a diagram in your explanation.

Let us suppose that there are 100 students at James' school. Also, let us suppose that all applied to both schools.
Then:

Private College   Public University
50   50

however:

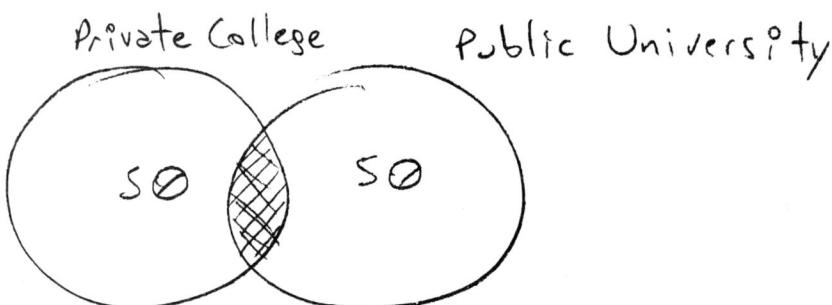

because there is no way of knowing how many students were accepted to <u>both</u> schools, it is impossible to be certain that James was accepted to either one. Now, if that number is zero, then James was accepted to one of the schools.

...1987 problem C

California Assessment Program — **score = 4** — *Survey of Academic Skills*

OPEN-ENDED MATHEMATICS QUESTION(S) — C

Name_____

Instructions: Use this sheet to answer the questions. Show as much of your work as possible. (In some cases, there may be more than one solution.) Use the reverse side of this sheet if needed.

James knows that half of the students from his school are accepted at the public university nearby. Also, half are accepted at the local private college. James thinks that this adds up to 100%, so he will surely be accepted at one or the other institution. Explain why James may be wrong. If possible, use a diagram in your explanation.

James may be wrong because:

take for example one student. He may be accepted at the public university, but he may also be accepted at the private college.

So half the school is accepted to the public university, but part of that half could also be included in the half that got accepted to the private college. So James might not be included in any of those groups.

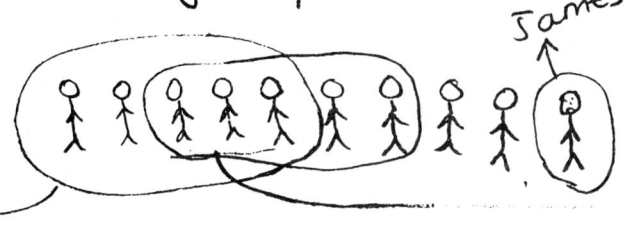

... 1987 problem D

California Assessment Program
score = 5
Survey of Academic Skills
OPEN-ENDED MATHEMATICS QUESTION(S)
D

Name_____

Instructions: Use this sheet to answer the questions. Show as much of your work as possible. (In some cases, there may be more than one solution.) Use the reverse side of this sheet if needed.

Consider the following problems.

A. Marla has a job after school. Last week she worked 2 hours and earned $10.50. How much did she earn per hour?

B. This week Marla worked 2 hours and earned $10.50 per hour. How much did she earn this week?

C. Marla worked two jobs. She earned $5.25 on the first and $10.50 on the second. How much did she earn altogether?

1. Which two problems are most similar and why?

    A & B

    Both are one job for using the same numbers.

    A. 10.50 ÷ 2
    B. 10.50 × 2
         ↑   ↑
    represents represents
    money   time (hours)

2. Which two problems are most dissimilar and why?

    B & C

    { B is one job
    { C is two jobs
    { B is $10.50 per hour
    { C is $10.50 per one job
    { A is $10.50 per week
    C does not use time at all.

...1987 problem D

California Assessment Program — **score = 4** — Survey of Academic Skills — **D**

OPEN-ENDED MATHEMATICS QUESTION(S)

Name_____

Instructions: Use this sheet to answer the questions. Show as much of your work as possible. (In some cases, there may be more than one solution.) Use the reverse side of this sheet if needed.

Consider the following problems.

A. Maria has a job after school. Last week she worked 2 hours and earned $10.50. How much did she earn per hour?

B. This week Maria worked 2 hours and earned $10.50 per hour. How much did she earn this week?

C. Maria worked two jobs. She earned $5.25 on the first and $10.50 on the second. How much did she earn altogether?

A: $5.25
B: $21.00
C: $15.75

1. Which two problems are most similar and why?

Problems C and B are most alike because addition is needed in figuring the both of them out.

example:
10.50   10.50
10.50   5.25
21.00   15.75

*Both equal the total she earned after she worked.

2. Which two problems are most dissimilar and why?

Problems A and C are most different because in problem A. you must find the total she earned per hour and in problem C., you need to just figure out her total earnings for both jobs together.

...1987 problem E

California Assessment Program   **score = 6**   *Survey of Academic Skills*   **E**

OPEN-ENDED MATHEMATICS QUESTION(S)

Name_____

Instructions: Use this sheet to answer the questions. Show as much of your work as possible. (In some cases, there may be more than one solution.) Use the reverse side of this sheet if needed.

The square shown below has sides of length 2 units. Connect the midpoints of the sides of the square, in order, to form an interior square. Repeat the same process to make squares within squares.

a) Draw the first five <u>interior</u> squares.

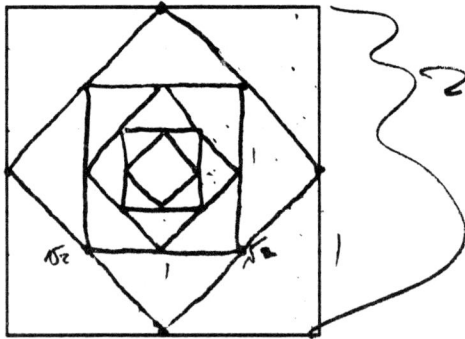

b) Write the sequence of numbers that represent the areas of the first five <u>interior</u> squares.

$$2, 1, \tfrac{1}{2}, \tfrac{1}{4}, \tfrac{1}{8}$$

c) What rule can be used to find the area of the nth <u>interior</u> square?

area of $n = \tfrac{1}{2}$ (area of $n-1$)

or

area of $n = \dfrac{1}{2^{(n-2)}}$

...1987 problem E

California Assessment Program

score = **3**

OPEN-ENDED MATHEMATICS QUESTION(S)

Survey of Academic Skills

E

Name_____

Instructions: Use this sheet to answer the questions. Show as much of your work as possible. (In some cases, there may be more than one solution.) Use the reverse side of this sheet if needed.

The square shown below has sides of length 2 units. Connect the midpoints of the sides of the square, in order, to form an interior square. Repeat the same process to make squares within squares.

a) Draw the first five <u>interior</u> squares.

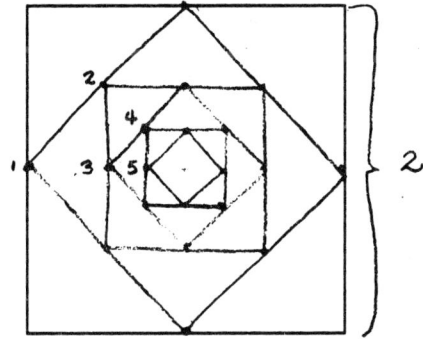

b) Write the sequence of numbers that represent the areas of the first five <u>interior</u> squares.

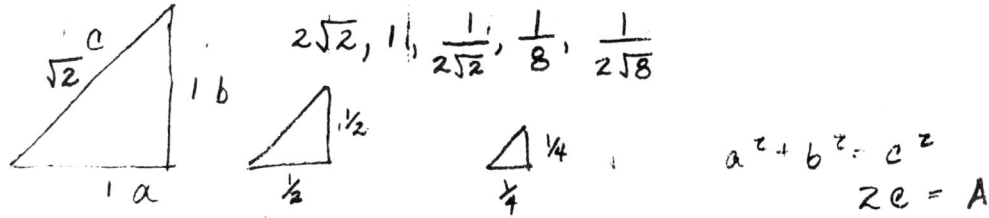

$2\sqrt{2}, 1, \frac{1}{2\sqrt{2}}, \frac{1}{8}, \frac{1}{2\sqrt{8}}$

$a^2 + b^2 = c^2$

$2c = A$

c) What rule can be used to find the area of the nth <u>interior</u> square?

$2c = A$ of the nth interior square

63

...1988 problem A

Sample Scored 1988 Responses

California Assessment Program 1988-89

score = 6

Survey of Academic Skills

A

OPEN-ENDED MATHEMATICS QUESTION(S)

Name _____ Sex *Female* Date of Birth *4-9-71*
School _____ District _____

Instructions: Use this sheet to answer the questions. Show as much of your work as possible. (In some cases, there may be more than one solution.) Use the reverse side of this sheet if needed.

The origin, O, and point A on this graph represent opposite vertices of a rectangle whose area is 24 square inches.

A (4, 6)

a) List one set of possible coordinates of point A. **(4, 6)**

b) Keep one vertex at the origin and the opposite vertex in the first quadrant. Mark and label the coordinates of at least two more points that could be opposite vertices of rectangles of area 24 square inches. Explain why you chose these coordinates.

(6,4) (1,24) (24,1) (3,8) (8,3) (2,12) (12,2)

These are all of the whole number factors of 24.

c) How many other points in this quadrant would give you rectangles with an area of 24 square inches if O is one vertex and the points are opposite vertices of these rectangles? Explain your reasoning.

Infinite. The set of answers follows along the curve like this:

Unless the set of answers is open only to whole numbers; in which case the answers for "b" are all the possible answers (8).

For Teacher Use Only

...1988 problem A

California Assessment Program 1988-89

score = ⑤

OPEN-ENDED MATHEMATICS QUESTION(S)

Survey of Academic Skills

A

Name _____ Sex __M__ Date of Birth __8/12/71__
School _____ District _____

Instructions: Use this sheet to answer the questions. Show as much of your work as possible. (In some cases, there may be more than one solution.) Use the reverse side of this sheet if needed.

The origin, O, and point A on this graph represent opposite vertices of a rectangle whose area is 24 square inches.

a) List one set of possible coordinates of point A. **(4,6)**

b) Keep one vertex at the origin and the opposite vertex in the first quadrant. Mark and label the coordinates of at least two more points that could be opposite vertices of rectangles of area 24 square inches. Explain why you chose these coordinates.

The area is equal to length times width. Thus, if one vertex of the rectangle is at the origin, the product of the x and y coordinates of the opposite vertex will equal the area, which is 24. The first quadrant has points with positive x and y values.

c) How many other points in this quadrant would give you rectangles with an area of 24 square inches if O is one vertex and the points are opposite vertices of these rectangles? Explain your reasoning.

An infinite amount. The values for x and y could be determined by the equation xy = 24. There are an infinite number of points that fit in between the points of the curve.

For Teacher Use Only

. . .1988 problem B

score = 6

California Assessment Program 1988-89
OPEN-ENDED MATHEMATICS QUESTION(S)

B

Survey of Academic Skills

Name _____ Sex __F__ Date of Birth __May 28, 1971__
School _____ District _____

Instructions: Use this sheet to answer the questions. Show as much of your work as possible. (In some cases, there may be more than one solution.) Use the reverse side of this sheet if needed.

You are a clerk in a garden shop. A customer comes to you for advice about his garden.

The customer has had a rectangular shaped vegetable garden for several years. The length of the fence around it was 90 feet. He found, by experience, that he uses a 100-pound bag of fertilizer on the garden each year.

This spring, the customer tore down the old fence and threw it away. He decided to enlarge the size of his garden and make another rectangular garden with a fence of length 180 feet. He was not sure how much fertilizer he should buy.

You, the clerk, are aware that the amount of fertilizer needed will depend on the size of the original and the new garden. Explain to the customer how he can find the number of bags of fertilizer needed for his new garden. Give some examples of possible dimensions of last year's and this year's garden in your explanation. You may want to use diagrams to help you explain.

P = 90   A = 506.25   100 lbs
P = 180 A = 2025

Sir, I assume that your original garden held the maximum area possible with a fence length of 90 ft. Likewise for your current garden. That maximum area is obtained by shaping the garden in a square. If the perimeter of your garden is 90 ft and it is in a square shape the area must be $(\frac{90}{4})^2$, that is, the length of one side $(\frac{90}{4})$ times the length of another side (all sides being of equal length). This area can be found to equal 506.25 ft². Now, if you know that you need 100 lbs. of fertilizer for every 506.25 ft², you need only to find the area of the new garden and see how many times 506.25 ft² will fit into it and buy 100 lbs. of fertilizer for every time it is divisible by that number. If the current garden is a square each side must be $\frac{180}{4}$ or 45 ft. 45 × 45 (one length times another length) is 2025 ft². 2025 ft² divided by 506.25 ft² is equal to 4. Therefore, you must buy 400 lbs. of fertilizer. OK?

For Teacher Use Only

...1988 problem B

California Assessment Program 1988-89

score = 4

Survey of Academic Skills

OPEN-ENDED MATHEMATICS QUESTION(S)

B

Name _____ Sex __MALE__ Date of Birth __7 JUNE 1972__
School _____ District _____

Instructions: Use this sheet to answer the questions. Show as much of your work as possible. (In some cases, there may be more than one solution.) Use the reverse side of this sheet if needed.

You are a clerk in a garden shop. A customer comes to you for advice about his garden.

The customer has had a rectangular shaped vegetable garden for several years. The length of the fence around it was 90 feet. He found, by experience, that he uses a 100-pound bag of fertilizer on the garden each year.

This spring, the customer tore down the old fence and threw it away. He decided to enlarge the size of his garden and make another rectangular garden with a fence of length 180 feet. He was not sure how much fertilizer he should buy.

You, the clerk, are aware that the amount of fertilizer needed will depend on the size of the original and the new garden. Explain to the customer how he can find the number of bags of fertilizer needed for his new garden. Give some examples of possible dimensions of last year's and this year's garden in your explanation. You may want to use diagrams to help you explain.

last years — 25 × 20, P = 90 ft, 100 pd needed
this year's — 50 × 40, P = 180, ? - needed

$20 \times 25 = 500$ sq ft $40 \times 50 = 2000$

$$\frac{500}{100} = \frac{2000}{x} \quad \cdot 100x$$

$500x = 200000$
$5x = 2000$
$x = \underline{400}$ pd of fertilizer (at most) this year compared to 100 pd last year.

$1 \times 90 = 90$
$1 \times 180 = 180$

$$\frac{90}{100} = \frac{180}{x} \quad \cdot 100x$$

$90x = 18000$
$9x = 1800$
$x = \underline{200}$

and at least 200 pd compared to 100 pd last year.

For Teacher Use Only

...1988 problem C

California Assessment Program 1988-89

score = 5

Survey of Academic Skills

OPEN-ENDED MATHEMATICS QUESTION(S)

Name _____ Sex M Date of Birth 3/21/71
School _____ District VSD

Instructions: Use this sheet to answer the questions. Show as much of your work as possible. (In some cases, there may be more than one solution.) Use the reverse side of this sheet if needed.

You have a bag of 30 identical wooden cubes.

a) If you spread the cubes out on a table, how many of the cubes would you need to completely cover the largest possible square surface on the table? Draw a diagram.

5 × 5 = 25 cubes

b) What is the largest possible cube you can make from the 30 cubes? Explain why this is the largest possible cube.

a $3 \cdot 3 \cdot 3 = 3^3 = 27$

to keep it a cube (equal on all sides) a 4^3 would be larger but there aren't enough blocks.

c) How would you determine the largest cube that could be made from N identical small cubes?

$(\text{\# of blocks})^3 \leq N$

$\sqrt[3]{N}$ = real positive integer

For Teacher Use Only

...1988 problem C

C

California Assessment Program 1988-89

score = ①

Survey of Academic Skills

OPEN-ENDED MATHEMATICS QUESTION(S)

Name _____ Sex __Male__ Date of Birth __05/01/71__
School _____ District __Unified S.D.__

Instructions: Use this sheet to answer the questions. Show as much of your work as possible. (In some cases, there may be more than one solution.) Use the reverse side of this sheet if needed.

You have a bag of 30 identical wooden cubes.

a) If you spread the cubes out on a table, how many of the cubes would you need to completely cover the largest possible square surface on the table? Draw a diagram.

It depends on the size of the table. It varies greatly.

b) What is the largest possible cube you can make from the 30 cubes? Explain why this is the largest possible cube.

It can't be determined from the information given, however the cube would be 30 times larger than the original cubes.

c) How would you determine the largest cube that could be made from N identical small cubes?

Find the lengths and/or areas of the original small cubes and multiply that by the number of small cubes.

For Teacher Use Only

...1988 problem D

California Assessment Program 1988-89
OPEN-ENDED MATHEMATICS QUESTION(S)

score = **4**

Survey of Academic Skills

D

Name _____ Sex __F__ Date of Birth __1/31/71__
School _____ District _____

Instructions: Use this sheet to answer the questions. Show as much of your work as possible. (In some cases, there may be more than one solution.) Use the reverse side of this sheet if needed.

Writing Situation

You and a good friend Sheila were shopping in a grocery store for food and beverages for a picnic. When you were buying soda, you noticed that you could buy it in quart (32 oz.) bottles or in six-packs of 12 oz. bottles. The six-pack cost $1.49, and the quart bottle cost $0.73. Sheila suggested buying two quart bottles, because it would be cheaper. Being thrifty, you took out your pocket calculator and in a few seconds said you should buy the six-pack because you get more soda per dollar. Sheila was impressed and asked how you knew that.

Instructions for Writing

Tell Sheila how you knew that the six-pack of soda was a better value than two quart bottles. Explain your method so that Sheila will understand why your calculations were valid and how she can make the same kind of calculation whenever she is in a similar situation.

$$2\,qts \times \frac{32\,oz}{1\,qt} = 64\,oz \quad 1.46\,\$ \quad \frac{64\,oz}{1.46\,\$} = 43.83\,oz/\$$$

$$6\,pack \times 12\,oz = 72\,oz \quad 1.49\,\$ \quad \frac{72\,oz}{1.49\,\$} = 48.32\,oz/\$$$

→ To buy 2 quarts (64 oz.) it would cost 1.46 $

∴ 43.83 ounces/per $

→ To buy a six pack (72 oz.) it would cost 1.49 $

∴ 48.32 ounces/per $

Therefore, you are getting a better deal if you buy the six pack because you pay less money for each quart.

For Teacher Use Only

...1988 problem D

score = 2

Survey of Academic Skills

OPEN-ENDED MATHEMATICS QUESTION(S)

Name _____ Sex __Female__ Date of Birth __9/23/71__
School _____ District __Unified District__

Instructions: Use this sheet to answer the questions. Show as much of your work as possible. (In some cases, there may be more than one solution.) Use the reverse side of this sheet if needed.

Writing Situation

You and a good friend Sheila were shopping in a grocery store for food and beverages for a picnic. When you were buying soda, you noticed that you could buy it in quart (32 oz.) bottles or in six-packs of 12 oz. bottles. The six-pack cost $1.49, and the quart bottle cost $0.73. Sheila suggested buying two quart bottles, because it would be cheaper. Being thrifty, you took out your pocket calculator and in a few seconds said you should buy the six-pack because you get more soda per dollar. Sheila was impressed and asked how you knew that.

Instructions for Writing

Tell Sheila how you knew that the six-pack of soda was a better value than two quart bottles. Explain your method so that Sheila will understand why your calculations were valid and how she can make the same kind of calculation whenever she is in a similar situation.

Divide # of ounces by price & figure out price per ounce. The six pack has 72 oz. for $1.49 while the quart size (buying 2) gives you 64 oz. for $1.46. The price of 2 quarts is almost equal to the price of the six pack except that you get more cola in 72 oz. than in 64 oz.

For Teacher Use Only

...1988 problem E

California Assessment Program 1988-89

score = 6

Survey of Academic Skills

E

OPEN-ENDED MATHEMATICS QUESTION(S)

Name _____ Sex __female__ Date of Birth __9-18-71__
School _____ District __450__

Instructions: Use this sheet to answer the questions. Show as much of your work as possible. (In some cases, there may be more than one solution.) Use the reverse side of this sheet if needed.

John has four place settings of dishes, with each place setting being a plate, a cup, and a saucer. He has a place setting in each of four colors: green, yellow, blue, and red. John wants to know the probability of a cup, saucer, and plate being the same color if he chooses the dishes randomly while setting the table.

Explain to John how to determine the probability of a cup, saucer, and plate being the same color. Use a diagram or chart in your explanation.

4 cups	4 saucers	4 plates				
green	green	green	x_1	x_2	x_3	x_4
yellow	yellow	yellow	y_1	y_2	y_3	y_4
blue	blue	blue	z_1	z_2	z_3	z_4
red	red	red				

pick a cup, chances of getting one of the four colors, 1 in 1
pick a saucer, chances of getting that same color, 1 in 4
pick a plate, chances of getting that same color, 1 in 4

$$\frac{1}{1} \cdot \frac{1}{4} \cdot \frac{1}{4} = \frac{1}{16} \cdot \frac{4}{1}$$ chances of getting a set of the same color = 1 in 4

four sets = four chances

For Teacher Use Only

...1988 problem E

score = ③

OPEN-ENDED MATHEMATICS QUESTION(S)

Survey of Academic Skills

E

Name _____ Sex __F__ Date of Birth __8/14/71__
School _____ District _____

Instructions: Use this sheet to answer the questions. Show as much of your work as possible. (In some cases, there may be more than one solution.) Use the reverse side of this sheet if needed.

John has four place settings of dishes, with each place setting being a plate, a cup, and a saucer. He has a place setting in each of four colors: green, yellow, blue, and red. John wants to know the probability of a cup, saucer, and plate being the same color if he chooses the dishes randomly while setting the table.

Explain to John how to determine the probability of a cup, saucer, and plate being the same color. Use a diagram or chart in your explanation.

First choose a cup. If it is Red, you want a Red saucer, so figure you have a 25% chance of choosing a Red saucer. Then you need to choose a Red plate. You have 25% chance of choosing a Red plate.

The probability of choosing a cup, then a saucer, then a plate of the same color =

½ (25%) = 12.5%

% chance choosing

	Plate	Saucer	Cup
Red	X	25%	25%
Yellow		25%	25%
Green		25%	25%
Blue		25%	25%

For Teacher Use Only

73

Additional Open-ended Problems

Problem 1.

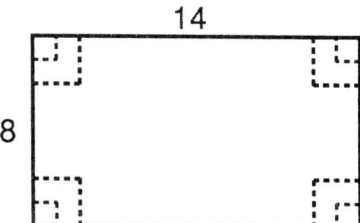 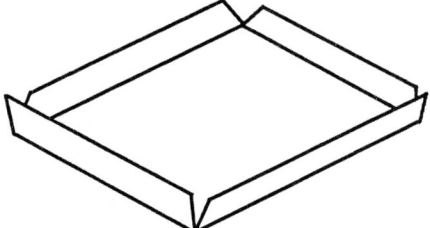

Henry wants to make a box from an 8 inch by 14 inch piece of cardboard. By cutting the same-sized square from each corner, he can fold up the sides to make a box, as shown.

If he cuts out only squares with whole-number sides, what is the volume of each box he can make?

If he is not restricted to whole-number squares, is there any larger box he can make from the cardboard? Explain.

Problem 2.

(a) Draw three rectangles of different lengths and widths, each with a perimeter of 36 units. Determine the area of each of the three rectangles.

(b) Determine the length and the width of the rectangle that would have the greatest area. Use a chart or graph to justify your answer.

Problem 3.

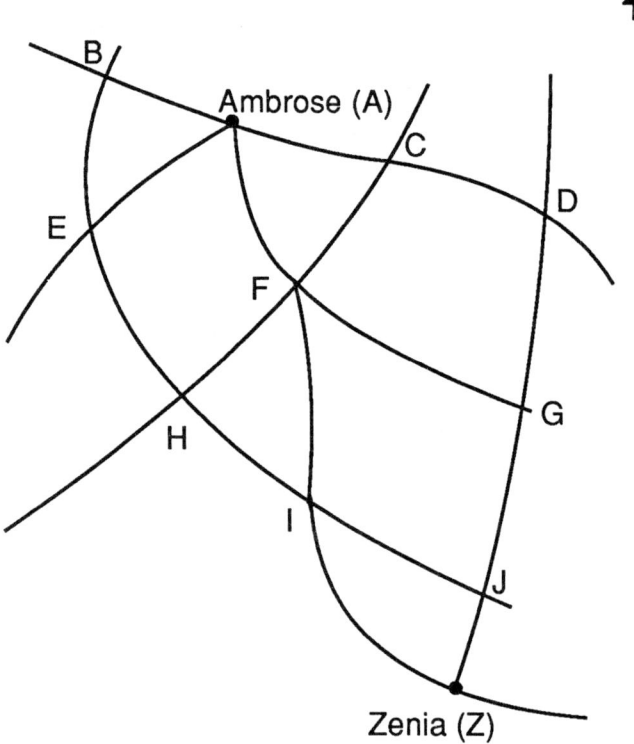

Mona wishes to drive from Ambrose (A) to Zenia (Z). She wants to know how many trips she can make to Zenia, using a different route each time. With the help of the road map given, show how she can systematically determine these routes if she must always be traveling in a southerly direction.

Problem 4.

Suppose that a running track is designed with two semicircular ends and two parallel straightaways of 100 yards or more, as shown below.

If the perimeter of the track is to be exactly 440 yards, explain how you would decide how long the straightaways should be and what the resulting diameter of the semicircles would be.

Problem 5.

Room 15 has 8 tables that measure 3 feet by 6 feet each. The tables are made so that they have to be fastened together in one of three ways:

When all of the eight tables are fastened together, how could they be arranged to give maximum seating? Draw a sketch and explain why you think this arrangement gives the most seating.

Problem 6.

Name	Favorite sport	Age	Grade in school	No. of brothers and sisters
Jack	Tennis	16	10	2
Sean	Tennis	18	12	1
Pete	Baseball	17	12	3
Maria	Golf	16	11	2
Kate	Tennis	17	12	1
Sara	Baseball	17	11	2
José	Football	15	10	4
Hushi	Crew	18	12	3
Bob				

Which person in the group is unique? Why?

When a new student, Bob, arrives at school and data are collected, it is discovered that information about him is closest to that for a typical student. Complete the chart by showing the data for Bob, and explain how you arrived at your choices.

Problem 7.

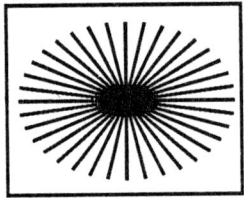
Fig. I

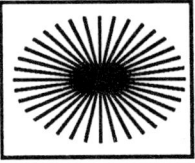
Fig. II

John took the picture shown on the left (Figure I) to the copy machine to make a copy. He didn't notice that someone had left the machine set for a reduction to 80 percent of original size (setting: .80). He gave the original picture away before he realized that he had actually made a reduced copy (Figure II).

(a) Write an explanation telling John what setting he would have to set on the copy machine to obtain from his reduced copy a picture with the original dimensions.

(b) What setting would he have to set on the copy machine to obtain from his reduced copy an enlargement that was 20 percent greater than the size of the original picture?

Problem 8.

Writing Situation

Your school club can sell either hot chocolate or cold cider at the concert but not both. The club buys both drinks for 50 cents per cup and sells them for $1.00 per cup. In warm weather clubs sell an average of 300 cups of hot chocolate or 400 cups of cold cider. In cold weather they sell an average of 700 cups of hot chocolate or 600 cups of cider.

Your club wants to make maximum profit, but the weather is unreliable. You don't know whether it will be warm or cold on the day of the concert. Your club has asked you for advice on whether to sell hot chocolate or cold cider.

Instructions for Writing

Tell your club which drink you think they should sell. Explain why your choice is the best one, considering the unreliability of the weather. You may want to use tables or diagrams to help explain your choice.

Problem 9.

At a party a cake is cut as follows:

Kim takes $\frac{1}{6}$ of the cake;

Bill takes $\frac{1}{5}$ of what remains of the cake;

Connie takes $\frac{1}{4}$ of what remains;

Antonio takes $\frac{1}{3}$ of what remains;

Keiko takes $\frac{1}{2}$ of what remains;

Jamal takes the remainder.

Draw a diagram of the cake:

1. How large is Jamal's piece of cake compared with Kim's? Explain your answer. You might want to refer to your diagram in your explanation.

Now assume there are n people at a party. The first person takes $\frac{1}{n}$ of the cake. The next person takes $\frac{1}{n-1}$ of what remains, then $\frac{1}{n-2}$ of what remains, and so forth, until the next to the last person takes $\frac{1}{2}$ of what remains.

2. How large is the last piece of cake compared with the size of the first piece?

3. Consider how the relative size of the piece of cake changes with successive cuts of the cake. Write a general statement about this situation that explains the relationship between the sizes of the pieces if you divide the cake this way.

Publications Available from the Department of Education

This publication is one of over 600 that are available from the California Department of Education. Some of the more recent publications or those most widely used are the following:

ISBN	Title (Date of publication)	Price
0-8011-0973-6	The American Indian: Yesterday, Today, and Tomorrow (1991)	$5.00
0-8011-0071-2	Assessment of Writing Performance of California High School Seniors (1977)	2.75
0-8011-0890-x	Bilingual Education Handbook: A Handbook for Designing Instruction for LEP Students (1990)	4.25
0-8011-0972-8	California Assessment Program: A Sampler of Mathematics Assessment (1991)	4.00
0-8011-0687-7	The California CBO: The 1987-88 Profile of Chief Business Officials in California Schools, K–12 (1989)	4.50
0-8011-0862-4	California Education Summit: Background and Final Report (a set) (1990)	5.00
0-8011-0889-6	California Private School Directory (1990)	14.00
0-8011-0924-8	California Public School Directory (1991)	14.00
0-8011-0748-2	California School Accounting Manual (1988)	8.00
	California's Daily Food Guide (brochure) (1990)*	6.00/25
0-8011-0874-8	The Changing History–Social Science Curriculum: A Booklet for Parents (1990)†	5.00/10
0-8011-0867-5	The Changing Language Arts Curriculum: A Booklet for Parents (1990)†	5.00/10
0-8011-0928-0	The Changing Language Arts Curriculum: A Booklet for Parents (Spanish Edition) (1991)†	5.00/10
0-8011-0777-6	The Changing Mathematics Curriculum: A Booklet for Parents (1989)†	5.00/10
0-8011-0891-8	The Changing Mathematics Curriculum: A Booklet for Parents (Spanish Edition) (1991)†	5.00/10
0-8011-0978-7	Course Models for the History–Social Science Framework, Grade Five—United States History and Geography: Making a New Nation (1991)	7.00
0-8011-0797-0	Desktop Publishing Guidelines (1989)	4.00
0-8011-0833-0	Directory of Microcomputer Software for School Business Administration (1990)	7.50
0-8011-0976-0	Economic Education Mandate: Handbook for Survival (1991)	7.00
0-8011-0856-x	English as a Second Language Handbook for Adult Education Instructors (1990)	4.50
0-8011-0041-0	English–Language Arts Framework for California Public Schools (1987)	3.75
0-8011-0927-2	English–Language Arts Model Curriculum Standards: Grades Nine Through Twelve (1991)	4.50
0-8011-0894-2	Enhancing Opportunities for Students Underrepresented in Higher Education	3.50
0-8011-0751-2	First Moves: Welcoming a Child to a New Caregiving Setting (videocassette and guide) (1988)‡	65.00
0-8011-0839-x	Flexible, Fearful, or Feisty: The Different Temperaments of Infants and Toddlers (videocassette and guide) (1990)‡	65.00
0-8011-0804-7	Foreign Language Framework for California Public Schools (1989)	5.50
0-8011-0809-8	Getting In Tune: Creating Nurturing Relationships with Infants and Toddlers (videocassette and guide) (1990)‡	65.00
0-8011-0875-6	Handbook for Contracting with Nonpublic Schools for Exceptional Individuals (1990)	8.00
0-8011-0824-1	Handbook for Teaching Cantonese-Speaking Students (1989)§	4.50
0-8011-0909-4	Handbook on California Education for Language Minority Parents—Portuguese/English Edition (1990)‖	3.25
0-8011-0734-2	Here They Come: Ready or Not—Report of the School Readiness Task Force (Full Report) (1988)	4.25
0-8011-0712-1	History–Social Science Framework for California Public Schools (1988)	6.00
0-8011-0782-2	Images: A Workbook for Enhancing Self-esteem and Promoting Career Preparation, Especially for Black Girls (1988)	6.00
0-8011-0750-4	Infant/Toddler Caregiving: An Annotated Guide to Media Training Materials (1989)	8.75
0-8011-0878-0	Infant/Toddler Caregiving: A Guide to Creating Partnerships with Parents (1990)	8.25
0-8011-0877-2	Infant/Toddler Caregiving: A Guide to Routines (1990)	8.25
0-8011-0879-9	Infant/Toddler Caregiving: A Guide to Setting Up Environments (1990)	8.25
0-8011-0876-4	Infant/Toddler Caregiving: A Guide to Social–Emotional Growth and Socialization (1990)	8.25
0-8011-0828-4	Instructor's Behind-the-Wheel Guide for California's Bus Driver's Training Course (1989)	20.00
0-8011-0869-1	It's Not Just Routine: Feeding, Diapering, and Napping Infants and Toddlers (videocassette and guide) (1990)‡	65.00
0-8011-0892-6	Literature for History–Social Science, Kindergarten Through Grade Eight (1991)	5.25
0-8011-0358-4	Mathematics Framework for California Public Schools (1985)	3.75
0-8011-0929-9	Model Curriculum Standards, Grades Nine Through Twelve (1985)	5.50
0-8011-0968-x	Moral and Civic Education and Teaching About Religion (1991 Revised Edition)	3.25
0-8011-0969-8	Not Schools Alone: Guidelines for Schools and Communities to Prevent the Use of Tobacco, Alcohol, and Other Drugs Among Children and Youth (1991)	3.25
0-8011-0974-4	Parent Involvement Programs in California Public Schools (1991)	6.00
0-8011-0845-4	Physical Education Model Curriculum Standards, Grades Nine Through Twelve (1991)	4.50

*The price for 100 brochures is $16.50; the price for 1,000 brochures is $145.00.
†The price for 100 booklets is $30.00; the price for 1,000 booklets is $230.00. A set of one of each of the parent booklets in English is $3.00.
‡Videocassette also available in Chinese (Cantonese) and Spanish at the same price.
§Also available at the same price for students who speak Japanese, Pilipino, and Portuguese.
‖The following editions are also available at the same price: Armenian/English, Cambodian/English, Chinese/English, Hmong/English, Japanese/English, Korean/English, Laotian/English, Pilipino/English, Samoan/English, Spanish/English, and Vietnamese/English.

ISBN	Title (Date of publication)	Price
0-8011-0886-1	Program Guidelines for Individuals Who Are Deaf-Blind (1990)	$6.00
0-8011-0817-9	Program Guidelines for Language, Speech, and Hearing Specialists Providing Designated Instruction and Services (1989)	6.00
0-8011-0899-3	Quality Criteria for Elementary Schools: Planning, Implementing, Self-Study, and Program Quality Review (1990)	4.50
0-8011-0906-x	Quality Criteria for High Schools (1990)	4.50
0-8011-0905-1	Quality Criteria for Middle Grades (1990)	4.50
0-8011-0815-2	A Question of Thinking: A First Look at Students' Performance on Open-ended Questions in Mathematics (1989)	6.00
0-8011-0858-6	Readings for Teachers of United States History and Government (1990)	3.25
0-8011-0831-4	Recommended Literature, Grades Nine Through Twelve (1990)	4.50
0-8011-0863-2	Recommended Readings in Literature, Kindergarten Through Grade Eight, Addendum (1990)	3.00
0-8011-0745-8	Recommended Readings in Literature, Kindergarten Through Grade Eight, Annotated Edition (1988)*	4.50
0-8011-0895-0	Recommended Readings in Spanish Literature: Kindergarten Through Grade Eight (1991)	3.25
0-8011-0753-9	Respectfully Yours: Magda Gerber's Approach to Professional Infant/Toddler Care (videocassette and guide) (1988)†	65.00
0-8011-0911-6	Schools for the Twenty-first Century (1990)	3.75
0-8011-0870-5	Science Framework for California Public Schools (1990)	6.50
0-8011-0665-6	Science Model Curriculum Guide, K–8 (1988)	3.75
0-8011-0926-4	Seeing Fractions: A Unit for the Upper Elementary Grades (1991)	7.00
0-8011-0752-0	Space to Grow: Creating a Child Care Environment for Infants and Toddlers (videocassette and guide) (1988)†	65.00
0-8011-0855-1	Strengthening the Arts in California Schools: A Design for the Future (1990)	4.50
0-8011-0920-5	Suggested Copyright Policy and Guidelines for California's School Districts (1991)‡	3.00
0-8011-0778-4	Survey of Academic Skills: Grade 12, Rationale and Content for English–Language Arts (1989)	2.75
0-8011-0785-7	Survey of Academic Skills: Grade 8, Rationale and Content for Mathematics (1989)	2.75
0-8011-0808-x	Survey of Academic Skills: Grade 12, Rationale and Content for Mathematics (1989)	2.50
0-8011-0739-3	Survey of Academic Skills: Grade 8, Rationale and Content for Science (1988)	2.75
0-8011-0266-9	Survey of Basic Skills: Grade 3—Rationale and Content (1985)	3.75
0-8011-0267-7	Survey of Basic Skills: Grade 6—Rationale and Content (1985)	3.75
0-8011-0140-9	Technical Assistance Guide for Proficiency Assessment (1979)	3.25
0-8011-0827-6	Technical Assistance Manual for the California Model School Accountability Report Card (1989)	3.75
0-8011-0904-3	Thinking Through Writing (1989)	3.50/each
0-8011-9952-2	Thinking Through Writing (1989)	17.00/10
0-8011-0846-2	Toward a State of Esteem: The Final Report of the California Task Force to Promote Self-esteem and Personal and Social Responsibility (1990)	4.25
0-8011-0854-3	Toward a State of Esteem, Appendixes to (1990)	4.25
0-8011-0805-5	Visual and Performing Arts Framework for California Public Schools (1989)	6.00
0-8011-0814-4	Writing Achievement of California Eighth Graders: A First Look (1989)	5.00
0-8011-0832-2	Writing Achievement of California Eighth Graders: Year Two (1989)	4.00
0-8011-0887-x	Writing Assessment Handbook, Grade 8 (1990)	8.50

*Includes complimentary copy of *Addendum* (ISBN 0-8011-0863-2).
†Videocassette also available in Chinese (Cantonese) and Spanish at the same price.
‡Also available in quantities of 10 for $12.50; 50 for $55.00; and 100 for $100.00.

Orders should be directed to:

California Department of Education
P.O. Box 271
Sacramento, CA 95812-0271

Please include the International Standard Book Number (ISBN) for each title ordered.

Remittance or purchase order must accompany order. Purchase orders without checks are accepted only from governmental agencies. Sales tax should be added to all orders from California purchasers. Stated prices will be in effect until June, 1992, and include shipping charges to anywhere in the United States.

A complete list of publications available from the Department, including apprenticeship instructional materials, may be obtained by writing to the address listed above or by calling (916) 445-1260.